21世纪英语专业系列教材

国际交流事务系列丛书　总主编 肖 肃

INTERNATIONAL CONFERENCE

国际会议

（英汉双语版）

谌华侨　/主编

图书在版编目(CIP)数据

国际会议:英汉双语版/肖肃总主编;谌华侨主编. —北京:北京大学出版社,
2018.4
(21世纪英语专业系列教材)
ISBN 978-7-301-26292-4

Ⅰ.①国… Ⅱ.①肖… ②谌… Ⅲ.①国际会议—英语—高等学校—教材
Ⅳ.①D813

中国版本图书馆CIP数据核字(2018)第009938号

书　　名	国际会议(英汉双语版)
	GUOJI HUIYI
著作责任者	肖　肃　总主编　谌华侨　主编
责任编辑	李　颖
标准书号	ISBN 978-7-301-26292-4
出版发行	北京大学出版社
地　　址	北京市海淀区成府路205号　100871
网　　址	http://www.pup.cn　　新浪微博:@北京大学出版社
电子信箱	evalee1770@sina.cn
电　　话	邮购部 62752015　发行部 62750672　编辑部 62754382
印刷者	北京宏伟双华印刷有限公司
经销者	新华书店
	720毫米×1020毫米　16开本　14.25印张　400千字
	2018年4月第1版　2018年4月第1次印刷
定　　价	48.00元

未经许可,不得以任何方式复制或抄袭本书之部分或全部内容。
版权所有,侵权必究
举报电话: 010-62752024　电子信箱: fd@pup.pku.edu.cn
图书如有印装质量问题,请与出版部联系,电话: 010-62756370

序一

四川外国语大学秉承"外语内核,多元发展"的办学特色定位,一直在积极探索建设适应国家和地方发展需求、服务国家对外开放事业的特色学科专业。我校国际关系学院以提高质量为根本、内涵发展为核心、凝练特色为抓手、适应需求为导向,积极探索融合外交学、国际关系和英语及部分非通用语种等外语专业为一体,培养"国际事务导向,外语与专业能力并重"的复合型人才,实现人才培养"打通学科、按需发展、追求卓越"的目标。

当今世界,中国正在作为一个世界大国和强国崛起,国家的发展对高校人才培养提出了更高、更全面、更多元的要求。对于外语院校而言,过去那种单一专业、单一方向、单一目标、封闭式的人才培养模式已明显不能适应时代的需求。有鉴于此,近年来,我校国际关系学院把培养"厚基础、宽口径、强能力、高素养、复合型"的"大外语"类国际交流型人才作为自己的奋斗目标,大力建设和发展跨外语及其他专业的融合性课程体系和相应师资团队,大力开展国际合作办学,积极推动素质和能力导向的教育教学改革,长期坚持适需对路的教材体系建设,以学生为中心、以学习为重心,为学生倾力打造各种课内、课外学习平台,如外交外事实验教学平台、模拟联合国大会活动、外交风采大赛活动、模拟APEC活动、中外合作办学项目、国际组织人才实验班等等,形成能有力保障教学和学习,富有特色的人才培养平台体系。

"国际交流事务系列丛书"正是在这样的背景下应运而生,是国际关系学院教育教学改革和特色教材建设的重要成果之一。

国际关系学院教师们编写的"国际交流事务系列丛书"是根据这些年教师们课程改革和教学实践的经验,结合国家发展战略和外交外事实践,采用英汉双语模式编写而成的。目前完成编写的有《国际礼仪》《国际会议》《国际公关》《外交谈判》和《国际社交文书写作》五本教材。这套丛书旨在通过对外交实务的学习和体验,逐步实现业务技能的提升;同时对发展学生的英语能力,特别是专门用途英语能力也十分有帮助。

  由于国际关系学院的人才培养模式还在不断探索和改革中,作为改革的成果,"国际交流事务系列丛书"难免存在一些不足,还需要在改革中不断地完善。但瑕不掩瑜,探索精神难能可贵。

  作为同行和同事,与丛书编写团队共勉——路漫漫其修远兮,吾将上下而求索!

四川外国语大学副校长

王鲁男

序二

中华人民共和国成立初期,周总理对中国外交人员的基本素质提出了"站稳立场、掌握政策、熟悉业务、严守纪律"的十六字方针,成为我国培养外交、外事人才的目标要求。

四川外国语大学国际关系学院年轻教师编写的"国际交流事务系列丛书"无疑践行了十六字方针的内容。丛书体现出来的国际规范、中国特色是站稳立场的表现,形态多样的正反案例是对掌握政策的具体阐释,双语特色是业务能力的一种体现,为此而展开的讨论则体现了学术无禁区、讨论有底线,诠释了外交外事工作的纪律。

《中华人民共和国国民经济和社会发展第十三个五年规划纲要》指出,"如期实现全面建成小康社会奋斗目标,推动经济社会持续健康发展,必须遵循坚持统筹国内国际两个大局。全方位对外开放是发展的必然要求。必须坚持打开国门搞建设,既立足国内,充分运用我国资源、市场、制度等优势,又重视国内国际经济联动效应,积极应对外部环境变化,更好利用两个市场、两种资源,推动互利共赢、共同发展。"当下,举国上下正掀起学习和讨论"十三五"纲要精神的热潮。

笔者曾经先后在外向型企业和高等学校教学一线工作多年,随后转战外交第一线,担任驻外大使、总领事,如今重回高校工作,深感国际事务导向、语言能力并重的国际化人才对于当下中国的意义。国际化人才是事关中华民族伟大复兴,实现"两个一百年"目标的智力资源。"国际交流事务系列丛书"则是中国国际化人才培养上的一次积极尝试,它将为中国的国际化人才培养提供一种新视角。该套丛书着眼于外交事务中的重大事项,通过形态多样的案例来展现外交、外事工作,既有明显的学术性,也有较强的可操作性,不仅易于在校学员学习,也是在职外交、外事人员的有益读物。

欣闻该丛书付梓,是为序。

外交学院党委书记

袁南生

Preface

前　言

国际会议是国家间处理国际事务的最普遍方式，如何进行国际会议关乎国际事务的有效解决。

本教材一改传统仅仅从理论上探讨国际会议的一般原则，或纯粹从事务方面来描述国际会议的承办细节所存在的问题，通过正反、中英双语案例对比来探讨中外国际会议操作性异同，以实现"融通国际规范，兼具中国特色"的国际会议实务原则。

同时，选择中英文反面案例进行拓展阅读，增加对所学国际规范的理解，以实现"国际事务导向，语言能力并重"的培养目标。

最后，根据时代发展的需要，采用国内外重大会议以及编者亲身经历和承办的国际会议作为练习题素材，编制了多样化的试题，以便于读者实现对所学内容的操作性诉求。

本教材通过满足高校和相关从业人员对于承办国际会议的操作性需求，来满足高校相关专业国际会议实务教学和相关领域职业培训的急切需求。

本教材提供国际会议的核心办会情境，再现国内外承办国际会议的真实过程，尝试改变人文社会科学教学过程中过多依赖教师单方面讲授的弊端，探寻人文社会科学实验教学的有效发展模式。

本教材的编写得到四川外国语大学学校层面和国际关系学院层面诸多领导和同事的帮助，他们不仅为教材的编写提供了专业指导，还为编写活动提供了大量支持。北京大学出版社也为教材的及时出版提供了大量专业指导。何琴和郝楠分别参与到基础知识和案例部分的资料整理过程中来，为教材早日成形贡献了力量。在教材付梓之际，特向上述机构和个人表示感谢。

本教材在编撰过程中，参阅了诸多中外相似题材的参考资料，因为篇幅所限，书中并未一一列举，在此一并表示感谢。

作为一种尝试，本教材或许在诸多方面存在不足或错误，期待读者的积极反馈，您的批评是我们改进该教材的不竭动力！

编　者

2017年9月

Contents
目 录

Chapter 1　Planning of International Conference
　　国际会议筹划 ………………………………………………………… 1
　Overview 内容概览 …………………………………………………… 1
　1. Basic Knowledge 基础知识 ………………………………………… 2
　　1.1 Introduction of International Conference 国际会议基础 ………… 2
　　1.2 The Planning of International Conference 国际会议筹划 ……… 4
　　1.3 Model of International Conference Planning
　　　　国际会议筹划理论模型 ………………………………………… 6
　　1.4 Contents of International Conference Planning
　　　　国际会议筹划内容 ……………………………………………… 7
　　1.5 Agenda of International Conference 国际会议议程 …………… 8
　2. Case Study 案例分析 ……………………………………………… 9
　　2.1 Case Summary 案例概述 ……………………………………… 9
　　2.2 13th International Conference on Meson-Nucleon Physics and the
　　　　Structure of the Nucleon ……………………………………… 9
　　2.3 第十三届国际茶文化研讨会暨中国（贵州·遵义）国际茶产业博览
　　　　会 ………………………………………………………………… 13
　　2.4 Case Comparison 案例对比 …………………………………… 16
　3. Supplementary Reading 拓展阅读 ………………………………… 17
　　3.1 The Organization of Conference ……………………………… 17
　　3.2 北京申办2022年冬奥会 ………………………………………… 21
　Exercises 课后练习 …………………………………………………… 22

Chapter 2　Catering Arrangement of International Conference
国际会议餐饮安排 …… 29
- Overview 内容概览 …… 29
- 1. Basic Knowledge 基础知识 …… 30
  - 1.1 Introduction of Catering Arrangement 餐饮安排基础 …… 30
  - 1.2 International Conference Catering Service Types
    国际会议餐饮服务种类 …… 31
  - 1.3 International Conference on Meal Planning Process
    国际会议餐饮计划流程 …… 32
  - 1.4 The Catering Arrangements of International Conferences
    国际会议餐饮安排 …… 33
  - 1.5 The International Conference Meal Budget 国际会议餐费预算 …… 35
- 2. Case Study 案例分析 …… 36
  - 2.1 Case Summary 案例概述 …… 36
  - 2.2 Brisbane's 2014 G20 Leaders' Summit …… 36
  - 2.3 2014年APEC领导人非正式会议 …… 38
  - 2.4 Case Comparison 案例对比 …… 41
- 3. Supplementary Reading 拓展阅读 …… 42
  - Catering in International Conferences …… 42
- Exercises 课后练习 …… 45

Chapter 3　Accommodation Arrangement of International Conference
国际会议住宿安排 …… 49
- Overview 内容概览 …… 49
- 1. Basic Knowledge 基础知识 …… 49
  - 1.1 Introduction of Accommodation 住宿基础 …… 49
  - 1.2 Factors 住宿安排影响因素 …… 51
  - 1.3 Process of Accommodation Arrangement 住宿安排流程 …… 51
- 2. Case Study 案例分析 …… 53
  - 2.1 Case Summary 案例概述 …… 53
  - 2.2 The Automatic Control and Artifical Intelligence Conference …… 53
  - 2.3 2008中国国际徽商大会 …… 56
  - 2.4 Case Comparison 案例对比 …… 59

3. Supplementary Reading 拓展阅读 ············ 60
      3.1 2012 London Olympics ············ 60
      3.2 雁栖湖 ············ 62
   Exercises 课后练习 ············ 64

**Chapter 4　Traffic Arrangement of International Conference
　　　　　　国际会议交通安排** ············ 73
   Overview 内容概览 ············ 73
   1. Basic Knowledge 基础知识 ············ 74
      1.1 Transport Security of International Conference
          国际会议交通保障 ············ 74
      1.2 International Conference Traffic Arrangement
          国际会议交通安排 ············ 74
      1.3 Pick-up Process 接机流程 ············ 75
      1.4 The Transport Costs of International Conference
          国际会议交通费用 ············ 76
   2. Case Study 案例分析 ············ 77
      2.1 Case Summary 案例概述 ············ 77
      2.2 2010 G8 Muskoka Summit ············ 77
      2.3 2008 徽商大会交通保障方案 ············ 80
      2.4 Case Comparison 案例对比 ············ 83
   3. Supplementary Reading 拓展阅读 ············ 85
      3.1 2009 Thailand ASEAN Summit ············ 85
      3.2 2015 亚欧商品贸易博览会交通保障方案 ············ 86
   Exercises 课后练习 ············ 88

**Chapter 5　The Media Publicity of International Conference
　　　　　　国际会议媒体宣传** ············ 94
   Overview 内容概览 ············ 94
   1. Basic Knowledge 基础知识 ············ 94
      1.1 Introduction of Media 媒体宣传基础 ············ 94
      1.2 Media Planning Process 媒体宣传计划流程 ············ 95
      1.3 Media Area 媒体采访区 ············ 97

3

2. Case Study 案例分析 ··· 98
   2.1 Case Summary 案例概述 ································ 98
   2.2 2014 International AIDS Conference ··············· 98
   2.3 关于举办2014中国边贸战略与发展高峰论坛暨26国国际
       投资峰会的通知 ·· 101
   2.4 Case Comparison 案例对比 ·························· 104
3. Supplementary Reading 拓展阅读 ····················· 105
   3.1 1936 Berlin Olympics ································ 105
   3.2 北京2008年奥运会场馆媒体中心 ················· 107
Exercises 课后练习 ··· 109

Chapter 6 The Marketing of International Conference
           国际会议市场开发 ·························· 115
Overview 内容概览 ··· 115
1. Basic Knowledge 基础知识 ····························· 115
   1.1 The Market Development of Conference 会议的市场开发 ····· 115
   1.2 Conference Marketing 会议营销 ··················· 118
2. Case Study 案例分析 ······································ 118
   2.1 Case Summary 案例概述 ····························· 118
   2.2 2015 Italy World Expo ································ 119
   2.3 2008北京奥运会市场开发计划 ····················· 123
   2.4 Case Comparison 案例对比 ·························· 126
3. Supplementary Reading 拓展阅读 ····················· 128
   3.1 Why We Must Protect Rio 2016 Official Brands ····· 128
   3.2 2014南京青奥会 ······································· 129
Exercises 课后练习 ··· 132

Chapter 7 The Registration of International Conference
           国际会议注册 ································ 136
Overview 内容概览 ··· 136
1. Basic Knowledge 基础知识 ····························· 136
   1.1 The Meaning of Registration 会议代表注册的意义 ····· 136
   1.2 Registration Method 代表注册方法 ················ 138
   1.3 Registry Arrangement 注册处布置 ················· 139

2. Case Study 案例分析 ·· 141
　　2.1 Case Summary 案例概述 ·································· 141
　　2.2 International Conference on Current Developments in
　　　　Statistical Sciences ·· 141
　　2.3 2014年第九届中国LNG国际会议 ····················· 143
　　2.4 Case Comparison 案例对比 ································ 146
3. Supplementary Reading 拓展阅读 ······························ 147
　　3.1 2015 Harvard Model United Nations Conference ······· 147
　　3.2 国外国际会议注册费 ·· 149
Exercises 课后练习 ·· 150

Chapter 8　The On-site Service of International Conference
国际会议会场服务 ··· **155**

Overview 内容概览 ·· 155
1. Basic Knowledge 基础知识 ·· 155
　　1.1 Guests Guide and Check-in 嘉宾引领和签到 ········ 155
　　1.2 Tea Break 茶歇 ·· 156
　　1.3 Conference Hall Arrangement 会场布置 ··············· 157
　　1.4 The Venue Management Work 会场管理工作 ······· 159
2. Case Study 案例分析 ·· 160
　　2.1 Case Summary 案例概述 ···································· 160
　　2.2 2015 Tokyo International Anime Fair ··················· 160
　　2.3 第九届中国（北京）国际园林博览会 ················ 163
　　2.4 Case Comparison 案例对比 ································ 167
3. Supplementary Reading 拓展阅读 ······························ 168
　　3.1 2010 G20 Seoul Summit ······································ 168
　　3.2 国际会议翻译 ··· 169
Exercises 课后练习 ·· 170

Chapter 9　The Venue Selection of International Conference
国际会议会场保障 ··· **174**

Overview 内容概览 ·· 174
1. Basic Knowledge 基础知识 ·· 174
　　1.1 The Venue Selection Criteria 会场选择的标准 ······· 174

  1.2 Venue Selection Steps 会场选择的步骤 …………………… 175
  1.3 The Content of Selecting the International Conference Center
    国际会议会场选择的内容 ……………………………… 176
 2. Case Study 案例分析 ……………………………………… 180
  2.1 Case Summary 案例概述 …………………………… 180
  2.2 2015 Tokyo International Anime Fair ……………… 180
  2.3 重塑蓝天：空气质量管理国际研讨会 ……………… 185
  2.4 Case Comparison 案例对比 ………………………… 188
 3. Supplementary Reading 拓展阅读 ……………………… 189
  3.1 2010 South Africa FIFA World Cup ………………… 189
  3.2 巴西世界杯 …………………………………………… 191
 Exercises 课后练习 ………………………………………… 193

Chapter 10 The Security of International Conference
国际会议安保 ……………………………………………… 195

Overview 内容概览 ……………………………………………… 195
 1. Basic Knowledge 基础知识 ………………………………… 195
  1.1 The Introduction of Security 安保基础 …………… 195
  1.2 The Measures of Security Plan 制订安保计划的步骤 … 196
  1.3 Security Program 安全保障方案 …………………… 196
  1.4 Emergency Treatment in Meeting 会议中突发事件的处理 … 198
 2. Case Study 案例分析 ……………………………………… 200
  2.1 Case Summary 案例概述 …………………………… 200
  2.2 2014 G20 Brisbane Summit Safety and Security Act (extract) … 201
  2.3 2014 上海亚信峰会 …………………………………… 204
  2.4 Case Comparison 案例对比 ………………………… 207
 3. Supplementary Reading 拓展阅读 ……………………… 208
  3.1 1972 Munich Olympics ……………………………… 208
  3.2 国际会议安保模式 …………………………………… 210
 Exercises 课后练习 ………………………………………… 211

Reference 参考文献 …………………………………………… 213

Planning of International Conference
国际会议筹划

Overview
内容概览

With the unfold of the modern era, international communications have become increasingly frequent. People have more opportunities to be involved in international conferences. The planning of the international conference is a prerequisite for international conferences, and is of great importance.

This chapter mainly comes up with some concepts and contents about international conference planning. Bilingual cases will be selected in order to show similarities and differences between Chinese and foreign international conference planning. Extended reading and recommended materials provide guidance for the interested reader. There are some exercises for students with regard to the issues dealt with in this chapter.

随着时代的发展,国家间交流合作日益频繁。国际会议在国际交流合作上扮演着越来越重要的角色。国际会议筹划是事关国际会议能够高效进行的前提条件,意义重大。

本章主要从宏观方面提出国际会议筹划的相关问题,设置主干知识,精选双语案例来展现中外国际会议筹划异同,并根据理论知识和双语案例提出实践操作中的重要问题,为读者提供关于国际会议筹划理论、案例和操作的全景图画。拓展阅读和推荐材料是对上述三大主题的延伸,为有兴趣的读者提供进一步学习的导引。

1. Basic Knowledge
基础知识

1.1 Introduction of International Conference 国际会议基础

With the development of modern society, interactions among states are far more frequent. International conferences play an increasingly important role in international cooperations. The first precondition of international conferences is the successful planning of it. In order to do so, we should clarify several important concepts related to international conferences:

Conference is a meeting of people who confer about a topic. An international conference is a meeting of people who come from different countries or regions to meet on some topics or goals. The following are different types of conferences:

Academic conference: A formal event, either scientific or academic, in which researchers present results, workshops and other activities.

Business conference: A conference which is organized to discuss business-related matters.

News conference: An announcement for the press (print, radio, television, etc.), with the expectation of questions, about the announced matter, etc.

Peace conference: A diplomatic meeting to end conflict.

Settlement conference: A meeting between the plaintiff and the respondent in a lawsuit, wherein, they try to settle their dispute without proceeding to trial.

Trade conference (or trade fair): A conference which is organized like a business conference but with a wider participation, which provides the opportunity for business people and the general public alike to network.

Definition of International Conference 国际会议的定义

现代汉语词典对会议的解释有两种,一种是有组织、有领导地商议事情的集会,另一种意思是一种经常商讨并处理重要事务的常设机构或组织。因此,会议是一些人为了某种目标而聚在一起,有组织有领导地商议事情的集会。

所谓国际会议,主要是指数国以上的代表为解决互相关心的国际问题、

国际会议筹划 | Planning of International Conference

协调彼此利益，在共同讨论的基础上寻求或采取共同行动（如通过决议、达成协议、签订条约等）而举行的集会。

Attributes of International Conference 国际会议的属性

National Subjectivity 国家主体性

国际会议的主体一般是主权国家。国家是国际会议上相互识别的主要标志和互相周旋的主要对象。换言之，每个与会者都具有某个国家的象征。不论与会者是国家正式派遣的代表，还是以个人身份与会，人们都会把与会者列在其所属国家名下，把与会者看成该国家的一部分。

Equivalence 对等性

国际会议最根本的原则是国与国之间的平等。正式的与会代表均享有同等的代表权和投票权。会议的时间、地点、议程、工作语言等应由与会者共同磋商决定。

Differences 差异性

国际会议因其举行规模及讨论问题的不同，往往有不同的组织形式。有些会议只有全体会议（即大会），许多会议则分为全体会议和小组会议，有时还设立特别委员会。

Non-violence 非暴力性

国际会议的方式是与会者就共同关心的问题进行讨论和交流，以达成共识。它是通过非暴力的方式来解决问题。它应当经过事先安排，讨论的内容应当预先得到确认和限定，并按照共同接受的议事规则行事。

Purpose 目的性

国际会议结束后一般会取得一些成果，其往往表现为会议文件，如决议、协议、声明、宣言、条约、和约或最后文件。当然，有时会议无法取得实质性效果。会议文件必须经过大会通过方才有效。对会议文件表示赞同的国家都应履行其应该承担的义务。国际会议的条约、和约一般须经各国代表签字，并得到法定数量国家批准后才能生效。

Classification of International Conference 国际会议的分类

按地理范围（the geographical scope）来分的话，国际会议可分为世界性会议、区域或地区会议、次区域会议。介乎这些类别之间还可有跨洲、跨区会议。

如果按会议的层次（The conference level）分，国际会议可分为国家元首会议、政府首脑会议、部长级会议、高级官员会议等。

3

如按会议周期(The conference cycle)分,国际会议可分为特别会议、例行会议和定期会议。

如按参加国(The participating countries)的数量,国际会议可分为双边会议和多边会议。

如按与会者有否官方身份(Identity)来判定,国际会议又可分为政府间会议和民间会议。

同时,也有人将例行会议排除在正式会议之外。这样,国际机构的年会、届会等都应视作非正式会议。基于不同的视角,根据不同的需要,可以对国际会议进行多种划分。

1.2 The Planning of International Conference 国际会议筹划

The planning of meeting is a prerequisite for the success of the conference. A complete international conference planning can generally be divided into five main aspects, each with its own specific requirements. These aspects are coordination, reception, public relations, meeting affairs, and security.

Coordination is the most important aspect. It means arranging the whole conference. Each stage of the conference is handled by a certain relevant agency or person. It contains the topic of the press conference, conference scale, conference guests, conference agenda, sponsors, and so on.

Reception refers to dinner, accommodation, and transportation. For dinner, such things as formality, time, flavors of food, etc. need to be considered. Accommodation is arranged according to the guests' level. It's necessary to book hotels that are convenient and comfortable. Preparing the cars and the proper route in advance is also necessary.

Public relations mainly concern journalism, broadcasting, and marketing. For large international conferences, media advertisement advocates the brand of the conference, city, or meeting sponsor. Therefore, the public relations module must be in the hands of professionals.

Meeting affairs include registration and conference services. The registration procedure confirms guests' information. Conference services must be polite and rule-based.

Security concerns venue and security. Because each type of international conference is different, the selection of a site is quite flexible. To ensure a

国际会议筹划 | Planning of International Conference

successful conference, each meeting should set up clear responsibilities, division of labor and security groups, and make a detailed security scheme and emergency action plan as well.

A reasonable and orderly international conference agenda is the key to the success of the conference, which is an important part of international conference planning. The international agenda plays a guiding role for the international conference planning.

Definition of International Conference Planning 国际会议筹划的定义

现代汉语词典中对筹划的解释为想办法，订计划。高级汉语字典中对筹划的解释为谋划。

会议筹划是指根据会议目的对会议制订整体的计划，涉及举办会议的各个部门和各种关系，由策划人将各种关系和矛盾重新调整，最后形成一套可行的方案。

所谓国际会议筹划，是指根据国际会议的目的对国际会议制订整体的计划，借助一定的科学方法和艺术，为决策、计划而构思、设计、制作策划方案以达到最终的会议效果。

Attributes of International Conference Planning 国际会议筹划的属性

（1）Integrity 整体性

国际会议筹划是对国际会议制订整体的计划，不是针对某一单独的环节制订的计划或安排。国际会议筹划是一个整体，不能缺少某些必要的环节。

（2）Nationality 国别性

正因为国际会议的参与者是国家代表，所以在不同的国家举办的国际会议的筹划有一定的差别。必须考虑到各国家之间的相似性和差异性，不能照搬其他国家的国际会议筹划模式。

（3）Pertinence 针对性

由于不同的国际会议有不同的目的，所以国际会议筹划需要有针对性。针对特定的会议议题和目的制定相应的筹划方案。

（4）Regularity 规律性

国际会议筹划有基本固定的策划模块和框架，有章可循。国际会议筹划可以借鉴其他类似的国际会议的筹划方案。

1.3 Model of International Conference Planning 国际会议筹划理论模型

The EMBOK is a three dimensional description of the knowledge and skills essential to create, develop and deliver an event. The term "event" includes conferences, exhibitions, festivals, special events, civic events, sports events and the like.

The aim of the International EMBOK Executive is "to create a framework of the knowledge and processes used in event management that may be customized to meet the needs of various cultures, governments, education programs, and organizations."

The EMBOK term for these areas is Knowledge Domains. Every event manager, from festival organizers to conference planners, must manage each of these areas. They represent the temporary Departments or Divisions of the event management.

The Domains can be subdivided as shown below. For the sake of symmetry the Domains are subdivided into seven Classes. The Classes can be further subdivided.

Note that the order of the classes does not imply their priority. Different types of events will have different priorities for each of the Classes.

A process is a series of step-by-step tasks or activities that are repeated in the management of an event. These actions can be regarded as the components in the overall process to deliver the event. Each action contributes towards the completion of a main task. Processes may be illustrated by a flow chart.

Processes acting on all areas of the EMBOK Domains include: Management, Analysis, Communication, Decision Optimization, Scheduling, and Risk Analysis.

Processes acting on specific areas of the EMBOK and/or on specific types of events include: Conference Registration, Press Accreditation , Site Choice, Procurement, Request for proposals, Costing, Engaging Speakers, and Contracting.

As with any project, the management of an event passes through a series of phases. Decisions on time underly all aspects of event management. The event is the deadline for most of the management. However, the event management

国际会议筹划 | PLANNING OF INTERNATIONAL CONFERENCE

does not end with the event. There remains the shutdown or closure phase.

After much discussion, the names for the phases decided by the EMBOK are: Initiation, Planning, Implementation, Event, and Closure.

During each phase the event team undertakes different tasks. The combination of knowledge, skills and processes is different. During the Initiation, for example, the event manager is studying the feasibility of the event. Once the event is found to be feasible, the Planning phase is entered.

The core values of the EMBOK framework are values that permeate all aspects of the event management process.

1.4 Contents of International Conference Planning 国际会议筹划内容

国际会议筹划的内容有五大板块,分别是统筹模块、接待模块、公关模块、会务模块和保障模块。

统筹模块主要是分工指挥,保证所有重要角色都有相关机构或人士来承担。首先应该确定会议主题、合作单位、会议规模、会议嘉宾邀请范围、会议议程、资金来源等几个方面的内容。

接待模块涉及餐饮、住宿、交通等几个方面。会议期间的餐饮安排需要关注的是餐饮形式、餐饮禁忌、餐饮时间,等等。住宿方面,要根据与会人员的级别确定住宿级别,选择住宿地点还要考虑价格是否合适、距离开会地点是否较近、交通是否方便、环境是否优美等问题。交通要提前安排好需要接待客人的车辆,制定最合适的路线,保障与会者可以按时安全到达,同时要制订相应的备用应急方案。

公关模块主要有两方面的内容,分别是新闻宣传和市场开发。对于大型国际会议而言,媒体宣传的最终目的是为了提升会议的品牌,同时形成会议举办地的城市品牌,或会议赞助商的企业品牌。因此,公关模块一定要由专业人士负责,负责人熟悉媒体运作的特点,能够进行精准的受众分析,制定出最易现实的、最易达成目标的传播策略。

会务模块包括注册和会场服务两方面。对于工作人员来说,办理会议注册既是确认嘉宾赴会的手续,又能在这一环节办理一些诸如信息确认、机票报销、材料发放工作。会场服务包括引领嘉宾就座、领导会见、同声传译耳机的发放与回收、会场管理等等。这些环节都要做到有礼有节,有章可循。

保障模块关注的是会场保障与会场安保问题。不同类型的国际会议,其选择的场地风格也不尽一致,需要考虑到会议场地的软硬条件是否符合会议要求。会场的确定要考虑会议规模、会议预算、交通便利性、会场设施和会议风格等几个方面。国际会议安全保卫工作的成功与否,事关主办方形象、经济发展和社会治安大局稳定,是对安保机构履行工作职责能力的一项考验。为确保国际会议的顺利进行,每次会议举办前都应该成立职责明确、分工仔细的安全保卫团体,制定详细的安保方案和应急解决方案。

1.5 Agenda of International Conference 国际会议议程

1.5.1 国际会议议程的定义

高级英汉词典将议程解释为会议期间议案讨论的程序。会议议程就是为使会议顺利召开所做的内容和程序工作,是会议需要遵循的程序。它包括两层含义,一是指会议的议事程序,二是指列入会议的各项议题。

所谓的国际会议议程,是指召开国际会议过程中所有议题性活动顺序的总体安排,不包括会议期间仪式性、辅助性的活动。

1.5.2 国际会议议程的属性

(1) Procedural 程序性。

会议议程的本质是一种程序,目的是使会议顺利召开,它分步骤完成。会议议程不是单独的某一阶段的安排,是从会议开始到会议结束的整个过程的框架性安排,以便于有顺序地进行各项活动。

(2) Concentrated 集中性。

会议议程不是独立分开的,它是所有会议议题的总和。会议议程集中了会议的重要环节,让参会者对本次会议的议题有清晰的认识。

(3) Non-unilateral 非单边性。

会议议程不是单方面制定的,是由多方面协商所确定的。国际会议涉及的会议议程是不同国家的代表人要参与的各项议题的总和,这里就涉及不同国家代表人想要争取的不同目标和利益。所以会议议程的设置必须是多方共同协商达成一致,并不是由某一国家代表单独决定其会议议程。

1.5.3 Composition 国际会议议程的构成

会议议程是一次会议上所要讨论的问题及其进行的程序。不同的国际会议,有不同的会议议程。通常国际会议议程有八个构成部分。

(1)开幕式;(2)选举会议主席;(3)通过议程;(4)大会发言;(5)分组讨论;(6)其他事项;(7)通过报告书;(8)闭幕式。

1.5.4 AGENDA

(1) Opening of the Conference;

(2) Election of the Chairman, the Vice-Chairmen and Reporter of the Conference;

(3) Adoption of the agenda;

(4) General Assembly speech;

(5) Group discussion;

(6) Other matters;

(7) Presentation of the conclusions of the work of the Conference by the Reporter General;

(8) Closure of the Conference.

2. Case Study 案例分析

2.1 Case Summary 案例概述

本章选择中文和英语两种语言,中外主办的国际会议两种策划方案,以便于读者理解中外在筹办国际会议时的异同。第一则是自然科学领域国际学术会议,主要用于展示国际上筹划国际会议的基本内容和方式。第二则是中国地方政府举办的国际会议,主要用以展示中国承办国际会议的主要内容和方式。

2.2 13th International Conference on Meson-Nucleon Physics and the Structure of the Nucleon

Case Guide-Reading 案例导读

This case is based on an international conference on physics, which intended to discover the panorama for an international academic conference. To illustrate the important information to the planning of this conference, such as the agencies, venue, it will be much more convenient for the reader to understand the essence and the characteristics of international conference. This case follows the inductive logic which obtains the general knowledge about the planning of the international conference through the single case.

1. Organizing Committee

Marco Battaglieri, INFN — Genova, Italy

Annalisa D'Angelo, Chair, University of Rome Tor Vergata / INFN — Roma Tor Vergata, Italy

Raffaella De Vita, INFN — Genova, Italy

Alessandro Pascolini, University of Padova / INFN — Padova, Italy

Giovanni Salmè, INFN — Roma, Italy

2. International Advisory Committee

Constantina Alexandrou, Univ. of Cyprus

Mauro Anselmino, INFN Turin

David Armstrong, College of William & Mary, Willamsburg (VA)

Angela Bracco, Univ. of Milan - Nupecc

Nora Brambilla, Univ. Munich

Stanley J. Brodsky, SLAC

Volker Burkert, Jlab

Simon Eidelman, Novosibirsk

HaiyanGao, DukeUniv.

Paola Gianotti, INFN-LNF

…

3. Circulars

First circular: February 2013

Second circular: 15 February 2013

Third circular: 12 May 2013

Fourth circular: 26 September 2013

4. Important Dates

January 2013: First Bulletin

February 15, 2013: Abstract Submission Begins

February 15, 2013: "Early Bird Registration" Begins

February 15, 2013: Hotel accommodation begins

February 15, 2013: Second Bulletin

国际会议筹划 | Planning of International Conference

April 15, 2013: Third Bulletin
…

5. Conference Venue

Pontificia Università della Santa Croce

Piazza di S. Apollinare, 49, 00186 Rome, Italy(the left picture)

The conference will take place at the Pontifical University of the Holy Cross, located in the center of Rome, behind the famous Piazza Navona. (the right picture)

6. Social Events — Conference Registration

The Conference Registration will take place on September 29 before 16: 30 to 19:30 at "Tempio di Adriano" Piazza di Pietra 91A. http://www.promoroma.com/pagina19_il-tempio-di-adriano.html

The temple is located at 8 minutes walk from the Conference Venue between Pantheon and famous Via del Corso.

A cocktail will be served during registration. Do not miss it!

7. Parallel Sessions

SUMMARY OF PARALLEL SESSIONS

ROOM	MONDAY	TUESDAY	WEDNESDAY	THURSDAY
	14:00 - 16:00			
Auditorium	Nucleon-Structure 1	Nucleon-Structure 3	Nucleon-Structure 5	Nucleon-Structure 7
305	Meson Spectroscopy 1	Meson Spectroscopy 3	Meson Spectroscopy 5	Meson Spectroscopy 7
306	Baryons 1	Baryons 3	Baryons 5	Baryons 8
307	Meson-Nucleon Systems 1	Meson-Nucleon Systems 3	Future Facilities 1	Future Facilities 3
308	Few Nucleons Systems 1	Fundamental Symmetries 1	Baryons 6	Fundamental Symmetries 4
	TEA BREAK 16:30 - 18:30			
Auditorium	Nucleon-Structure 2	Nucleon-Structure 4	Nucleon-Structure 6	
305	Meson Spectroscopy 2	Meson Spectroscopy 4	Meson Spectroscopy 6	
306	Baryons 2	Baryons 4	Baryons 7	
307	Meson-Nucleon Systems 2	Meson-Nucleon Systems 4	Future Facilities 2	
308	Few Nucleons Systems 2	Fundamental Symmetries 2	Fundamental Symmetries 3	

*该会议信息来源于其主页 http://menu2013.roma2.infn.it/

Analysis and Summary 分析概要

This case is selected from an English international conference which fully demonstrates the outline of it. The successful international conference that usually contains the following aspects: personnel, important procedure, venue, social event and agenda. Compared with international conference held in China, the important dates, conference venue and agenda are clear. The social events indicate the characteristics with the host city. This case is a typical representative of the planning of the international conference abroad.

Questions 思考题

1. What is the composition for the two committees in this conference? What are the features for the personnel? Does it have any differences from the international conference held in China?
2. Compared with the domestic conference, what are the features of the arrangement in this agenda?

国际会议筹划 | Planning of International Conference

2.3 第十三届国际茶文化研讨会暨中国(贵州·遵义)国际茶产业博览会

Case Guide-Reading 案例导读

本案例主要选择一则在中国举办的国际会议,以展现中国筹划国际会议的全貌,便于读者掌握中国策划国际会议的核心内容和特性,并明确国际会议的基本构成。

一、名称、主题及时间、地点
  (一)名称:
    第十三届国际茶文化研讨会暨中国(贵州·遵义)国际茶产业博览会
  (二)主题:
    复兴中华茶文化,振兴中国茶产业
  (三)时间:
    2014年5月28—29日(会期2天)
  (四)地点:
    贵州省遵义市湄潭县

二、举办单位
  (一)主办单位:
    贵州省人民政府、中国国际茶文化研究会、中国茶叶流通协会
  (二)承办单位:
    遵义市人民政府、贵州省农业委员会
  (三)协办单位:
    贵州茅台酒厂(集团)有限责任公司、贵州省茶文化研究会、贵州省茶叶协会、贵州省绿茶品牌发展促进会、贵州省茶叶学会
  (四)执行单位:
    湄潭县人民政府、遵义市农业委员会
  (五)协助执行单位:
    遵义市茶文化研究会、遵义市茶叶流通协会

三、主要活动内容
  (一)开幕式
  (二)招商引资签约仪式

（三）盛世兴茶——茶的深度开发和综合利用论坛
（四）中国国际茶文化研究会第五次会员代表大会
（五）茶与酒行业高端对话
（六）茶区考察活动
（七）贵州省第五届茶艺大赛及表演颁奖大会
（八）茶类产品、茶叶加工机械、茶食器皿展示展销活动
（九）万人品茗活动
（十）"圣地茶都·醉美遵义"图片展
（十一）新闻发布会
（主要活动详细内容省略）

四、组织机构

主任：
王×× 遵义市人民政府市长
刘×× 贵州省农业委员会主任

副主任：
孟×× 中共遵义市委副书记
胡×× 贵州省农业委员会常务副主任
范×× 遵义市人民政府常务副市长
……

成员：
杨×× 遵义市委副秘书长、市接待处处长
高×× 遵义市委副秘书长
杨×× 遵义市政府副秘书长
……
罗×× 遵义市农委主任
张×× 遵义市供销社主任
汪×× 遵义市发改委主任
……

筹委会办公室设在湄潭县中国茶城贵州生态茶文化博物馆三楼，胡××、田××同志兼任办公室主任，黄××同志兼任副主任，杨××、高××……等同志为成员。办公室从有关单位抽调专人办公，负责组织、协调、督促、落实各项工作。

国际会议筹划 | Planning of International Conference

筹委会办公室下设以下工作组：

（一）综合督导组

　　组长：黄×× 　　副组长：高××、周××……

　　工作职责：……

（二）宣传文艺组

　　组长：雷×× 　　副组长：余××、戴××、王××、牟××、程××

　　工作职责：……

（三）展会展览组

　　组长：陈×× 　　副组长：张××、梁××、卢××、沈××、张××

　　工作职责：……

（四）论坛论道组

　　组长：罗×× 　　副组长：周××

　　工作职责：……

（五）后勤保障组

　　组长：杨×× 　　常务副组长：陈×× 　　副组长：唐××、李××

　　工作职责：……

（六）茶区考察组

　　组长：李×× 　　副组长：向××

　　工作职责：……

（七）安全保卫组

　　组长：郑×× 　　副组长：杨××、王××

　　工作职责：……

（八）环境整治组

　　组长：杨×× 　　副组长：李××、赵××

　　工作职责：……

各工作组负责制定本组活动的具体实施方案，报筹委会办公室审定并组织实施。

五、筹备工作计划

第一阶段（4月30日前）：……

第二阶段（5月10日前）：……

第三阶段（5月15日前）：……

15

Analysis and Summary 分析概要

该案例选取一个中文国际会议策划作为样本,全面展现了中国举办国际会议的策划全貌。由该案例可以看出,中国策划国际会议时较为重视举办单位的构成、会议议程、组织机构这几方面的内容。其举办单位一般代表国际会议的级别,会议议程是会议内容的表现,组织机构体现了国际会议的重要性。该案例是中国筹划国际会议的典型代表之一。

Questions 思考题

1. 在该案例中,筹办国际会议时各举办单位之间有何关系?举办单位对国际会议顺利进行有何意义?
2. 在该案例的众多主要内容中,哪一项或几项最为重要?结合案例解释这些主要内容的重要性?
3. 中国筹办国际会议的组织机构有何特性?筹委会办公室在国际会议进行过程中扮演何种角色?

2.4 Case Comparison 案例对比

在分工指挥上,前者①由意大利 INFN 国家核物理研究所牵头主办,Pontificia Università 承办,设立组织委员会。后者由筹委会主体负责,设主任和副主任。设立筹委会办公室,下设综合督导组、宣传文艺组、展会展览组、论坛论道组、后勤保障组、茶区考察组、安全保卫组、环境整治组,各司其职。并且在每一阶段均有详细的计划安排。

在接待方面,前者餐饮和住宿按照会议指南的要求,参会人员自行预定,由入住酒店负责。根据会议指南提示,参会人员自行前往会议地点。后者的餐饮、住宿和交通均有会议承办方解决。

在会议公关方面,前者的新闻宣传由在场新闻记者负责,后者邀请国内外主要新闻媒体、中央驻黔新闻媒体负责人及记者 50 人参与会议报道。前者的会议市场开发通过旅行来实现,后者进行茶类产品、茶叶加工机械、茶食器皿展示展销活动来实现。

在会务方面,前者的会议注册在网上自主进行,参会人员需先行将会议期间所需材料上传到会议指定工作电脑上,会议期间的重要事项将刊登到

---

① 前者指 13th International Conference on Meson-Nucleon Physics and the Structure of the Nucleon,后者指第十三届国际茶文化研讨会暨中国(遵义)国际茶产业博览会。后续章节案例对比部分均采用此行文风格。

国际会议筹划 | Planning of International Conference

指定的刊物；后者的会务事宜由宣传文艺组、展会展览组、论坛论道组负责。

在会议保障方面，前者的会议将在 Pontifical University of the Holy Cross 举行；后者由后勤保障组负责参会人员的接送、报到、食宿安排和医疗救护、食品卫生监督，作好有关礼仪服务工作。在安保方面，前者提醒参会人员注意相关事项；后者由安全保卫组负责交通保畅、安全保卫、消防安全、维稳等工作。

Analysis and Summary 分析概要

根据国际会议内容构成的基本模块，案例对比将所选择的中文和英文案例分块进行比较，以突显中外筹划国际会议时各项具体工作的异同。

Questions 思考题

1. 通过上述两个案例的学习，可否明确国际会议筹划的主要内容？
2. 上述两份国际会议策划方案在几大模块上有何异同？
3. 上述两份国际会议策划方案中的不同模块构成内容有何内在异同？

3. Supplementary Reading 拓展阅读

3.1 The Organization of Conference

> The organization of a conference requires a similar strategic approach to that needed for planning and managing most other events. Clear objectives should be set from the beginning, a budget has to be established, a venue must be sourced and delegates' accommodation and travel arrangements made, and a programme has to be prepared and the conference managed for its duration. Increasingly, health and safety, security, venue contracts and service guarantees are, among a number of other aspects, needing serious consideration, but there is not enough space to cover these adequately here. Then, after the conference is over, final administrative details have to be completed and some evaluation of the conference should take place. While there are different factors to take into account when organizing a conference for 500 delegates rather than

one for 50, the essential components are the same.

Similar steps are required for the organization of other events, such as sporting events, concerts, celebrations and rallies, whether these are of national or international significance like the football World Cup Finals or the Olympic Games, or of more localized importance, such as an antiques fair or agricultural show.

Organizing conferences is a high-pressure activity, not recommended for those of a nervous disposition. Yet, well handled, it can be tremendously exhilarating and rewarding. It goes without saying that excellent organizational skills are a must, as are attention to detail and a willingness to work long and often irregular hours, especially in the immediate build-up period and during the event itself. Conferences need to be planned with the precision of a military operation. Indeed, it is not surprising that a number of those now working successfully as conference organizers have come from a military background. Cotterell (1994) suggests that:

A conference for 200 people for two or three days is likely to take up to 250 hours or around six normal working weeks, even without counting the two or three 18-hour days which will be needed just prior to the event.

In some cases, companies and organizations will already have systems in place when the event is, for example, an annual event which runs along similar lines year after year. In other cases, it may be an entirely new event for which no previous organizational history or tradition exists. Both scenarios have their advantages and disadvantages:

◆ The regularly-held conference may operate smoothly with just some fine tuning and updating to established systems and procedures. It might, however, be failing to achieve its real potential as a conference, having become staid and predictable, and it may be that a completely fresh approach would be beneficial. The challenge for a new organizer will be to revolutionise the organization of the conference without alienating too many of the staff or members (if it is a membership organization) associated with the previous régime.

国际会议筹划 | Planning of International Conference

> ◆ Where there is no previous event history, an organizer has the benefit of beginning with a clean sheet of paper. There are no set ways of doing things, no established contacts, no 'venues that we always use'. There is a freedom to bring something of his own identity to the event, to build up his own network of information and suppliers, and to ensure that the event management systems are put in place to his own design. But such freedom brings with it a responsibility which can appear daunting if the organizer has been thrust into the role of running a conference with minimal training and experience. This, regrettably, is still the position in which far too many conference organizers find themselves.

Digest from Tony Rogers, *Conferences and Conventions: A Global Industry (Second Edition)*, Elsevier Ltd., 2008.

Multiple Choices

Directions: In this part there is one incomplete sentence. For each sentence there are four choices marked from A to J. Choose the ANSWERS that best complete the sentence.

Which of the following steps is needed for a successful conferences?(　　)

A. Objective   B. Budget   C. Venue
D. Accommodation   E. Travel Arrangement   F. Programme
G. Conference Duration H. Health, Safety, and Security
I. Conference Service J. Conference Evaluation

Questions and Answers

Directions: In this part there are two questions. You need to ask the question based on the words or phrases from the passage.

Does the requirement for the organization of Rio 2016 Olympic Games differ from the CCTV Spring Festival Gala?

What is the special nature for the conference organizer?

19

Summarization

Directions: In this part there is one question, there are four choices marked from A to D. Choose the ONE answer that best completes the sentence.

What is the MAIN idea for the Cotterell's words? (   )

A. The conference is time-consuming job.
B. The conference is labour-intense field.
C. It is very necessary to well-prepare the conference.
D. The conference organizer needs to adjust to the irregular change.

Chart-filling

Directions: Complete each chart with appropriate words or phrases from the passage.

What are the main advantages and disadvantages for a new hand and veteran with the conference preparation?

Organizer	Advantages	Disadvantages
New Hand		
Veteran		

3.2 北京申办2022年冬奥会

北京申办2022年冬奥会的愿景

愿景：纯洁的冰雪·激情的约会

北京成功举办2008年奥运会和残奥会，为发展奥林匹克运动、传播奥林匹克精神做出了重要贡献，留下了丰厚的遗产。中国哈尔滨申办过2010年冬奥会，但冬奥会尚未在中国这个世界上人口最多的国家举办过。

冰雪是纯洁的象征，冰雪运动是充满激情和活力的运动。希望举办2022年冬奥会，打造纯洁的体育运动环境、自然生态环境和社会人文环境，推动冬季运动蓬勃发展。

邀请全世界不同信仰、不同肤色、不同种族的人们在中国欢聚一堂，共享奥林匹克带来的激情、欢乐与福祉。

北京申办2022年冬奥会的申办流程

时段	申办事项	时间点
第一阶段	各国家/地区奥委会通知国际奥委会申办城市名称	2013年11月14日
	签署《申办城市受理流程》	2013年12月1日
	2014年索契冬奥会观察员项目	2014年2月7—23日
	向国际奥委会提交申请文件和保证书	2014年3月14日
	国际奥委会及专家对所有答复进行审阅	2014年3月—6月
	在平昌召开索契2014总结会	2014年6月29—7月2日，7月4—5日
	确定2022年冬奥会候选城市	2014年7月7日
第二阶段	向国际奥委会提交申办报告及保证书	2015年1月
	国际奥委会评估委员会考察	2015年3月
	国际奥委会评估委员会报告	2015年5/6月
	向国际奥委会委员作候选城市陈述	2015年5/6月
	2022年冬奥会主办城市遴选	2015年7月31日

资料来源：北京2022年冬季奥林匹克运动会申办委员会官方网站

做图题

根据国际会议筹划的相关内容,将北京2022年冬季奥林匹克运动会申办流程转化为流程图。

基本要求:
1. 体现申办流程
2. 体现每个流程的时间
3. 流程图能提升运作和管理水平

计算题

根据流程图,计算申办流程总共需要多长时间?

思考题

1. 北京2022年冬季奥林匹克运动会的申办愿景对于本次比赛有何意义?

2. 本次冬季奥林匹克运动会的申办愿景与往届冬季奥林匹克运动会的申办愿景有何差异?

Exercises
课后练习

● **填空**

1. 阅读下列材料,将材料后的模块、问题填入相应备注信息前的空格中。

Sochi Olympics
The 2014 Winter Olympics, officially known as the XXII Olympic Winter Games, were a major international multi-sport event held in

国际会议筹划 | Planning of International Conference

Sochi, Russia, in the tradition of the Winter Olympic Games.

The Games were held from 7—23 February 2014, with opening rounds in certain events held on the eve of the opening ceremony, 6 February 2014. Both the Olympics and 2014 Winter Paralympics were organized by the Sochi Organizing Committee (SOC). Sochi was selected as the host city in July 2007, during the 119th IOC Session held in Guatemala City. It was the first Olympics in Russia since the breakup of the Soviet Union in 1991. The Soviet Union was the host nation for the 1980 Summer Olympics in Moscow.

A total of 98 events in 15 winter sport disciplines were held during the Games. A number of new competitions—a total of 12 accounting for gender—were held during the Games, including biathlon mixed relay, women's ski jumping, mixed-team figure skating, mixed-team luge, half-pipe skiing, ski and snowboard slopestyle, and snowboard parallel slalom. The events were held around two clusters of new venues: an Olympic Park constructed in Sochi's Imeretinsky Valley on the coast of the Black Sea, with Fisht Olympic Stadium, and the Games' indoor venues located within walking distance, and snow events in the resort settlement of Krasnaya Polyana.

In preparation, organizers focused on modernizing the telecommunications, electric power, and transportation infrastructures of the region. While originally budgeted at US$12 billion, various factors caused the budget to expand to over US$51 billion, surpassing the estimated $44 billion cost of the 2008 Summer Olympics in Beijing as the most expensive Olympics in history.

The lead-up to these Games was marked by several major controversies, including allegations that corruption among officials led to the aforementioned cost overruns, concerns for the safety of lesbian, gay, bisexual, and transgender (LGBT) athletes and spectators due to the effects of recently passed legislation, protests by ethnic Circassian activists over the site of Sochi (where they believe a genocide took place), and threats by jihadist groups tied to the insurgency in the North

Caucasus. However, following the closing ceremony, commentators evaluated Games to have been overall successful.

模块	问题	备注
		国际奥委会委员、国际滑雪联合会主席卡斯帕在接受瑞士电视台采访时透露了另一个负面消息：索契冬奥会筹备过程中，有超过1/3的筹备资金涉嫌被贪污，具体数目可能高达180亿美元。 　　俄罗斯反对派领袖、俄前总理鲍里斯·涅姆索夫则对媒体表示，俄罗斯政府用来举办冬奥会的250亿至300亿美元的资金被贪污。
		According to the report, *Yellow water, weird toilets and more problems at Sochi Olympics,* from INDYSTAR: Athletes' social media post the following messages: *There are bees in the honey* Yellow water that you can't use on your face *Strange bathroom rules* *Can't flush the toilet paper* *Also, the toilet seats are right next to each other* The water at Sochi (Photo: Via Twitter)

续表

模块	问题	备注
		According to *Sochi Olympics: Propaganda and Theft Amid PR "Disaster" for Putin* of New American: *Before the $51 billion games began, the increasingly discredited establishment media tried desperately to make the Sochi Olympics about homosexuals and a Russian law banning sexual propaganda to minors. The real stories, though, were largely overlooked — at least until Olympians began arriving with cameras and Twitter accounts. Now, as fears grow, the games are being variously portrayed as a joke, a propaganda stunt, a bonanza of corruption, and a serious danger — and in some cases, a testament to the supposed glory of former KGB man Vladimir Putin and the Russia he rules.*
		According to *Sochi Opening Ceremony glitch: only four of five rings light up* from Yahoo Sports: *As a fog-wreathed chorus dressed in traditional Russian costumes sang, five snowflakes rose gracefully above the stadium floor: And you could see what was coming next. Slowly but surely, the snowflakes began to transform: almost all of them did. And then we had a nearly-complete set of Olympic rings.*

续表

模块	问题	备注
		According to *The Sochi Olympic Games and the Threat of a Terrorist Attack. Who is Behind the Caucasus Terrorists* of Global Research: In the weeks leading up to the Sochi Winter Olympics, the Western Media have released a dribble of "trustworthy reports" examining "the likelihood" of a terrorist attack at the height of the Olympic games. In late January, the British government warned "that more terrorist attacks in Russia (following the Volgograd attack in December) are very likely to occur before or during the Winter Olympics in Sochi". (BBC, January 27, 2014). As the Olympic torch reaches Sochi, CNN released, in a timely fashion, the results of an "authoritative" opinion poll (based on a meager sample of 1000 individuals): "57% of Americans think terror attack likely at Sochi Games"

国际会议筹划 | Planning of International Conference

● 填空题

将下面的模块和问题填到上面表格的相应位置。

可供选择模块：　　　可供选择问题：
统筹模块　　　　　　Corruption
接待模块　　　　　　Yellow Water, Weird Toilets
公关模块　　　　　　Western Media Revelations
会务模块　　　　　　Only Four of Five Rings Light Up
保障模块　　　　　　Threat of Terrorist Attacks

● 问答

该部分有3题，根据相应的要求，回答问题。

1. 请根据所学国际关系和国际会议知识，列举古今中外5个知名国际会议，并用中英文表达其名称。

2. 根据所学国际会议知识，分析2014年亚太经合组织（APEC）领导人会议中所体现出的国际会议的国家主体性、非暴力性、对等性、差异性和目的性，并运用已经公开的新闻报道图片来具体阐述之。

   国家主体性——

   非暴力性——

   对等性——

   差异性——

   目的性——

   以联合国相关会议为案例，分析联合国框架下的国际会议分类，并用中英文表达其会议名称。

   地理范围——

   会议层次——

   会议周期——

   参会数量——

   与会者身份——

27

● 问答

阅读国际会议议程，回答问题

17th March, 2014 Arrival   Transfers to the hotels and registration of participants 19:00 — 21:30   Welcome Dinner: Hosted by (tbc)
18th March, 2014 09:00 — 10:00   Opening Session — Minister Marcelo Neri 10:00 — 10:30   Interval 10:30 — 12:30   Technical Session 1 — BRICS and their neighbors — trade and investment 12:30 — 14:30   Lunch 14:30 — 16:30   Technical Session 2 — Sustainable Inclusive Development 16:30 — 18:30   Technical Session 3 — ICTs and Innovation challenges in the BRICS Dinner hosted by (tbc)
19th March, 2014 09:00 — 11:00   Technical Session 4 — BRICS International Development Cooperation 11:30 — 13:30   Technical Session 5 — Productivity and the Middle Income Trap 13:30 — 15:00   Lunch 15:00 — 17:00   Technical Session 6 — Social Technologies 17:00 — 18:00   Discussion of main recommendations 19:30 — 21:30   Farewell Dinner
20th March, 2014 Touristic Activity

According to the requirement of the agenda, what is the problem of this conference?

If there is any problem for the agenda of the conference above, how can you improve it?

Catering Arrangement of International Conference
国际会议餐饮安排

Overview
内容概览

The service quality of the catering arrangement determines the participant's degree of satisfaction. Hence, it's urgent to promote the service quality of catering arrangement. The quality of the food is determined by features like presentation, portion size, smell, taste and texture.

This chapter looks at Introduction of Catering Arrangement, Service Types, Planning Process, and Budget.

It includes case studies on Brisbane's 2014 G20 Leaders' Summit, APEC informal leaders' meeting in 2014.

会议期间的工作用餐不仅是享用美食的场合,而且还是沟通与交流的重要时机,良好的餐饮服务会让与会者留下深刻印象。因此,应合理安排就餐时间、地点、餐饮形式,并及时收集餐后意见以便改进,就餐过程中应考虑到特殊的饮食习惯。国际会议餐饮安排的质量不仅影响国际会议本身的活动,还代表着一个国家的形象。因此,策划并办好国际会议的餐饮活动是国际会议成功举办的关键因素之一。

1. Basic Knowledge
基础知识

1.1 Introduction of Catering Arrangement 餐饮安排基础

The function of catering planning is to provide food, drink and accommodation at any time of the day or night for people of all ages, races, creeds and from all walks of life.

Conference planners should develop a theme and provide the atmosphere for each event. In addition to fine food and service, the catering services staff must also consider entertainment, props, decorations, and music.

The conference planning managers will have to determine methods of combining and presenting food and dishes that demonstrate originality and generate genuine interest and anticipation in the minds of the participants.

This market research can provide preliminary direction on probable users, concept, menu selections, hours of operation, style of service (such as table service versus self-service), size (number of seats and total square footage), and price points.

The Significance of International Conference Catering Services 国际会议餐饮服务的意义

餐饮服务是会议进行阶段中不可或缺的组成部分。就餐形式的合理安排有利于促进整个会议的顺利进行，进而达到会议目标。会议期间的每一次宴会都为与会者提供了增加认识和了解的机会，所以会议餐饮就成为会议期间人们交往不可或缺的环节。

国际会议餐饮服务的质量不仅影响国际会议本身，还影响主办城市或国家的形象。通过合理的餐饮安排，可以体现出一个国家的风俗文化、风土人情，展现一个国家的国家实力等。

The Principals of International Conference Banquets 国际会议宴请原则

（1）"4M"原则。

"4M"原则是在世界各国广泛受到重视的宴请礼仪原则。"4M"指的是4个以M为首的单词：菜单(Menu)、举止(Manner)、音乐(Music)和气氛

(Mood)。也就是说,在安排宴会活动时要讲究精美的菜单、优雅的举止、动听的音乐和热烈的气氛四方面。精美的菜单会给客人带来难忘的就餐经历,优雅的举止让客人体会到主人的良好修养,动听的音乐和热烈的气氛为宾主双方营造融洽的谈话氛围。

(2)适量原则。

适量原则即节约、务实。在宴请活动中,不论活动规模、参与人数、用餐档次,还是宴请的具体数量,都要从实际需要和实际能力出发,丰俭适度,量力而行。切忌虚荣攀比、铺张浪费。

1.2 International Conference Catering Service Types 国际会议餐饮服务种类

Catering service mainly has the following varieties during the time of international conferences. They are breakfast, coffee break, lunch and dinner.

A breakfast can be a complex or simple buffet. A rich variety of buffets allow guests to serve themselves.

The conference planners must also arrange two break times during the scheduled activities for that day. The time is generally chosen at about two hours after the conference has started. The benefit of the break is to give participants some relaxation time. They can walk around, relax, and relieve fatigue. And the break time should be confined to between fifteen and thirty minutes.

The buffet is always a suitable choice for the participant during a time consuming international conference.

The banquet includes a welcome dinner and a closing dinner. The reception is usually a meeting during the first meal, which is therefore also called a "welcome reception." The conference generally does not last longer than two hours. One should generally host the reception in the same venue as (or in a venue near) the conference so as to avoid a reception vehicle. The closing dinner is usually arranged the day before the end of the meeting in the evening or at the end of the meeting. The closing banquet usually chooses a table with ten people. After the best arrangement of theatrical performances, programs sometimes interest representatives. Theatrical performances should be limited to an hour or so; one can choose to have a performance featuring strong national characteristics and local characteristics; this performance typically signals the end of the party.

国际会议中的餐饮服务主要有以下几种：

（1）早餐 Breakfast。

早餐的选择范围很大，可以是正式早餐，也可以是自助早餐。品种多样的自助早餐会让人"各食所需"。早餐一般以清淡为主，不宜太油腻、麻辣等。

（2）茶歇 Coffee Break。

茶歇也称为间茶，每天可安排两次，上下午各一次，会议举行一个半小时或两个小时后开始进行。茶歇能让会议代表久坐之后四处走动，以放松身心，缓解疲劳。休息时间一般控制在15分钟到30分钟。

（3）会议午餐 Lunch。

会议午餐的标准不用太高，通常采用自助餐形式，不供应酒和其他饮料，但要提供汤或冰水。会议午餐时间可稍微长一点，可以分散就餐，避免拥挤。

（4）晚宴 Dinner。

宴会包括欢迎宴和闭幕宴会。招待会通常是会议的第一个餐饮活动，因此也称欢迎招待会。招待会可安排在会议正式开始的前一天晚上，也可以安排在正式会议的当天晚上。招待会的持续时间一般不超过两小时。招待会一般安排在会议场地内或者附近，尽量避免使用接待车辆。

闭幕晚宴通常安排在会议结束的前一天，或者在会议结束的当天晚上。大型会议的宴会也应尽量安排在会址内或会址附近。闭幕宴会通常选用桌餐，十人一桌，桌上摆设制作精美的菜单。最好在热菜上完之后安排文艺演出，丰富多彩的节目有时会引起代表的兴趣。文艺演出的时间应该控制在一小时左右，可以选择具有浓郁民族特色或者地方特色的节目，文艺演出结束后，可以宣布宴会结束。

1.3 International Conference on Meal Planning Process 国际会议餐饮计划流程

For per-person menus, a final guarantee of attendance is required five full working days prior to your event day.

The catering arrangement in the international conference has some procedures. The first step is to confirm the total volume of the representatives.

国际会议餐饮安排 | CATERING ARRANGEMENT OF INTERNATIONAL CONFERENCE

Contact forum guests in advance to confirm whether they will attend the international conference dinner or party in order to effectively arrange meal service.

The second step is to determine the method of dining. The conference catering arrangement usually has two forms. One is buffet; the other is service at the table. There are three categories: Chinese style, western-style, or hall style.

The third step is to confirm the level. All meals arrangement should be limited to the total budget. According to budget, the dining can be divided into the table and buffet.

Determining the Number of Diners 确定就餐人数

提前与参会嘉宾进行联系，确认其是否参加国际会议用餐或者宴会，统计出具体的人数，以方便安排餐食服务。

Determining the Dining Ways 确定就餐方式

会议餐饮安排通常有两种形式：自助餐和围桌餐。类别有三种，分别为中式、西式和清真式。

对于大型会议来说，会期通常持续两天或以上，这就需要安排嘉宾的早、中、晚餐。统一安排餐饮的会议，对于成本的控制非常重要，建议在确定就餐方式前与餐食服务商进行沟通，选择最为合理的类型。

Determining Meal Standards 确定餐标

所有的餐食安排要以预算可承受的限度为准，根据预算来制定用餐标准，分为桌餐标准和自助餐标准。

制定好餐标及餐谱，严格区分正式代表与随行人员、家属，特殊要求者可以和餐厅协商。自助餐一般可发餐券，围桌式餐饮安排需考虑以下几个方面：(1)开餐时间；(2)每桌人数；(3)入餐凭证；(4)席位安排；(5)特殊饮食习惯；(6)酒水种类等。

1.4 The Catering Arrangements of International Conferences 国际会议餐饮安排

Catering is a kind of service. Caterers must, at all times, seek to meet the customers' requirements. As participants come from a wide variety of countries. Different races may have social and religious requirements that are reflected in the request for certain foods or dishes.

Food is to be cooked and served well. It is important to be aware of the social and religious requirements of others, which is the responsibility of the caterers. Catering managers plan menus, obtain supplies, and supervise the preparation, cooking and service of the meals, and are also responsible for training and safety. Only the finest raw materials must be used, the production processes must be closely monitored.

Catering Service 餐饮服务

国际会议是国际交往的一大盛事,除了需要服务人员掌握基本的服务技能以外,还必须参与涉外礼仪培训、简单的口语培训、彩妆培训等等。为了服务人员能更好地服务大会,服务员们需要托着杯盘背靠墙壁或头顶书本练习站姿;男服务员要进行会场布置的培训,确保在规定时间内,所有桌椅板凳都在一条直线;而相对心细的女服务员则需要进行熨烫练习。

The Choice of Ingredients 食材的选择

为保证食品安全,准备餐饮的厨房最好实行门禁管理,配有食品运送专用梯,相关人员持卡并只有运送食物时才可乘坐。

为了保证食物质量,食材入库后专门进行清洗房,而蔬菜肉类也要抽检送进食品检验室,待检查完毕后,根据各个厨房的分工不同,分别送入水果、蔬菜、海鲜、肉类加工间等,经过择菜、清洗等步骤后,再送入相应厨房。

The Design of Menu 菜单的制定

设计菜单需考虑的因素包括季节、国别、地方特色和客人们品尝新口味的勇气。国际会议的点菜是门大学问,有以下几个原则:(1)冷热结合;(2)荤素搭配;(3)一种菜品不宜多次出现;(4)特色菜品;(5)分量足够;(6)美观大方。

在异国他乡举办会议,要体验当地美食,一个好办法是举办一次欢迎自助餐,上一些当地特色菜,并向客人介绍每道菜的原料和做法,或在盛菜的盘子上贴一张说明。会议期间,非常重要的一点是午餐能让客人们精神饱满地回到会场,精力充沛地继续下午的议程。也是出于这个考虑,午餐不宜提供酒水,而应提供诸如冰茶、柠檬水、果汁或纯净水等软饮料。

Special Arrangement 特殊安排

根据国际会议的惯例,所有菜品都将遵循"无猪肉"原则。据介绍,国际

国际会议餐饮安排 | Catering Arrangement of International Conference

会议餐饮中,来宾的文化习俗、宗教信仰、口味习惯各不相同,需要调和众口。为了照顾一些宗教习俗,并考虑到大部分宾客的习惯,一般而言,牛肉是使用频次最高的肉类原料。绝对不能使用野生动物。

在境外参会代表集中入住的酒店里,专门配备"指西针",方便信仰某宗教的代表在祈祷时辨别方向。

对于各国领导人的个人禁忌和口味喜好也要尽量照顾,会议召开前服务人员需要收集相关信息,在选择食材和调味方式时作为参考。

1.5 The International Conference Meal Budget 国际会议餐费预算

The conference budget mainly depends on the goal of conference and the needs of the conference agenda.

The catering budget includes costs for breakfast, lunch, alcohol and beverage, tea break, and dinner party.

The breakfast is usually a buffet. Buffet costs are proportion to the number of the participants.

The cost is basically according to the amount allocated for the budget, which put forward combination food, drink in the different periods.

A dance party budget may be more complicated than a regular party. If the party adheres to a set meal standard and scale, the budget is very easy to calculate. But if the reception/PROM budget involves site and program support, the organizers may need a longer time to confirm the budget.

会议的餐饮费用,主要取决于会议的目的和会议议程的需要。

会议策划者需要考虑的会议餐饮费用通常有早餐、中餐、晚餐、会场茶歇、联谊酒会/舞会。

Breakfast 早餐

早餐通常是自助餐,当然也可以采取围桌坐式就餐,费用按人数计算。(但考虑到会议就餐的特殊性及原材料的预备,所以预计就餐人数不得少于实际就餐人数的15%,否则餐厅有理由拒绝按实际就餐人数结算——而改为按预定人数收取费用)。

Lunch and Dinner 午餐及晚餐

午餐及晚餐基本属于正餐,可以采取按人数预算的自助餐形式,按桌预算的围桌式形式。如果主办方希望酒水消费自行采购而非由餐厅提供,餐

35

厅可能会收取一定数量的服务费用。

Coffee Break 会场茶歇

此项费用基本上是按人数预算的,预算时可提出不同时段茶歇的食物、饮料组合。承办者告知的茶歇价格通常包含服务人员费用;如果主办方需要非程序服务,可能需要额外的预算。

通常情况下,茶歇的种类可分为西式与中式两种:
(1) 西式基本上以咖啡、红茶、西式点心、水果等为主;
(2) 中式则以开水、绿茶或者花茶、果茶、水果、咖啡、水果及点心为主。

2. Case Study
案例分析

2.1 Case Summary 案例概述

本章选取澳大利亚和中国所承办的两次国际盛会来展现国际会议餐饮安排。通过中英双语向读者展现国内外国际会议安排的基本规范和最新发展趋向。第一则案例是澳大利亚在G20领导人峰会上别具匠心的烧烤安排,展现西餐,尤其是当地特色美食在国际会议中的独特作用。第二则案例是中国承办的APEC会议上的国宴安排,展现中国饮食文化的博大精深。

2.2 Brisbane's 2014 G20 Leaders' Summit

Case Guide-Reading 案例导读

This case is based on the catering arrangement of Brisbane's 2014 G20 Leaders' Summit, which was intended to discover the panorama for the catering arrangement of international conference. This case is cited to illustrate some main features of catering on current conference abroad.

> In November 2014, Brisbane hosted the Group of Twenty (G20) Leaders' Summit, the principal forum for international economic cooperation and decision-making. Over the days of the event, Brisbane was in the global spotlight, with leaders from the world's most influential economies gathering in the city. As an annual event, the G20 gives world

国际会议餐饮安排 | Catering Arrangement of International Conference

leaders the chance to share ideas and outline visions regarding key international issues.

G20 was held at the Brisbane Convention and Exhibition Centre (BCEC) South Bank on 15 and 16 November 2014. During this time international leaders, delegates and media were able to experience Brisbane's highlights.

G20 is the most significant international event held in Brisbane since the 1982 Commonwealth Games and Expo'88. It showcased Brisbane as a world class destination for business, tourism, education and events.

Preparations for the G20 Leaders' Summit spanned more than two years, with Brisbane City Council playing a role in delivering the event in partnership with the Australian and Queensland Governments.

The Prime Minister of Australia was the Chair of the G20 in 2014.

G20 attendees

The G20's permanent membership comprises of 19 of the world's most powerful countries plus the European Union. Guest countries included Singapore, New Zealand, Mauritania, Senegal and Myanmar. International organizations were also invited to attend.

The event attracted more than 4000 delegates and 3000 media representatives from around the world.

Food Arrangement

The Australian Barbecue is a huge tradition in Australian culture. This way of eating dates back to early white settlement as the weather definitely lends itself to outside eating. Most Australian households have a Barbecue of some sort, from the simple wood operated or gas type to the huge, top of the range outside oven styles.

In this summit, Australian Barbecue is served. The full menu for the Retreat barbecue is listed below.

Salads

Vannella buffalo mozzarella with heirloom tomatoes and basil

Barbecued new season asparagus, peas, broad beans and goats curd with Mount Zero wild olives

37

> Salad with kale, broccoli and avocado with toasted seeds
> **Seafood**
> Freshly shucked Moreton Bay rock oysters
> Cooked Mooloolaba king prawns with lime mayonnaise
> **Barbecue**
> Moreton Bay bugs, figs, pancetta and fresh bay kebabs with chimichurri
> Smoked and spiced Flinders Island butter flied leg of lamb with yoghurt and eggplant
> Crispy skin Tasmanian ocean trout, avocado, apple, radish and watercress salad
> **Dessert**
> Pavlova

Analysis and Summary 分析概要

This case is selected from G20 which fully demonstrates the outline of the catering arrangement for international conference. In this case, the catering arrangement reflects the traditional culture of Australia, which is carefully selected by the organizer. Those are major differences from the food arrangement in domestic conference in China. This case is a typical example for catering arrangement in international conference.

Questions 思考题

What is the composition of the food arrangement in this conference?

What are the features of the food in this conference?

Do they have any difference from those of the food in the international conference held in China?

2.3 2014年APEC领导人非正式会议

Case Guide-Reading 案例导读

本案例主要选择一则中国举办的国际会议，全面展现中国承办国际会议时的餐饮安排，以便于读者掌握中国主办国际会议的餐饮安排特性，并明确

国际会议餐饮安排 | CATERING Arrangement of International Conference

国际会议餐饮安排的基本构成。

　　2014年APEC会议是由亚太经济合作组织发起的会议，是继2001年上海举办后时隔13年再一次在中国举办，于11月中旬在北京召开，包含领导人非正式会议、部长级会议、高官会等系列会议。

　　此次峰会的主题是：共建面向未来的亚太伙伴关系。其中领导人峰会于2014年11月10日至11日在北京怀柔雁栖湖举行，中国国家主席习近平主持峰会。此次峰会是由上一任中国国家主席胡锦涛于2012年在俄罗斯举行的第二十次峰会上宣布的，决定由中方主办的2014年APEC领导人非正式会议。

会议地点

　　2014年亚太经合组织第22次领导人非正式会议，地点在北京怀柔雁栖湖。雁栖湖位于北京郊区怀柔城北8公里处的燕山脚下，北临雄伟的万里长城，南偎一望无际的华北平原，是一处风光旖旎的水上乐园。雁栖湖水面宽阔，湖水清澈，每年春秋两季常有成群的大雁来湖中栖息，故而得名。自1986年以来，怀柔区政府不断加大对雁栖湖的资金投入，陆续建成了一些景区，已经成为北京市民假期休闲旅游的好去处，2000年被国家旅游局评为国家AAAA级风景区。

　　北京雁栖湖生态发展示范核心区21平方公里中12套总统别墅、国际会议中心和一个精品酒店的主体结构，会议核心区将提前为各国参会人员创造便捷的居住和出行条件。

　　在陆路交通方面，岛上通过一座新建的上下两车道公路桥与外界相连。与新桥直接连接的范崎路正在进行加宽改造。除了陆路交通，上岛还可走水路或空中走廊。其中，同样处于建设群中的金雁饭店外形宛如新日初升，从雁栖湖东岸跃出地面，这里规划建设的小型港口可与雁栖岛上的酒店港口实现近距离通航；而岛上规划的直升机停机坪，将打开一条会议中心与外界直通的空中走廊。

会议议题

　　亚太经合组织(APEC)北京峰会经贸领域主要议题敲定，本次APEC领导人会议的主题是"共建面向未来的亚太伙伴关系"。在这个主题下有三个重要的议题：推动区域经济一体化、促进经济创新发展、改革与增长，加强全方位互联互通和基础设施建设。

餐饮保障

在北京召开的APEC峰会,餐桌上也京味十足,糖葫芦、驴打滚、宫廷小窝头等北京传统小吃都登上了菜单。本次APEC会议期间,这里预计开餐142场,接待就餐人数约7.3万人,还不包括为新闻中心提供的服务。

食材买来后,通过送货口就进入了国家会议中心总面积达7000平方米、分布在三个楼层的厨房。地下一层的厨房像一个巨大而管理森严的迷宫,实行门禁管理,配有食品运送专用梯,相关人员持卡并运送食物时才可以乘坐。中心还配有专门的食品检验室,并能将检验数据直接上传至北京市工商局、卫生局、食药局。

蔬菜、水果、肉类、海鲜等各类食材从送货口进来后,先抽样检验,再被分类送进各自的加工间接受粗加工、细加工,经过多道手续后,才到大厨手上做成各种美味。在水果加工间,苹果是逐个被工人手工洗净,再在15摄氏度的环境下切制加工的;在海鲜加工间,虾仁要逐个手工抽掉虾线。这里的鸡蛋进厨房前,要先被清洗消毒,以防禽流感。各类食材加工间里的案板和菜刀有好几种颜色。红案板是切肉的,黄案板是切禽类的,蓝案板是切海鲜的,绿案板是切蔬菜水果的;每种案板都有相同颜色的刀与之配套。

Analysis and Summary 分析概要

该案例选取的是一个由中国政府主办的国际会议的餐饮安排。通过分析该次会议的餐饮安排,读者容易发现中国方面在准备本次会议时餐饮安排的独到之处,体现了主办方的心意。该则案例体现出主办方在准备餐饮过程中的特殊保障措施,在就餐环境、餐饮准备过程中的特性。该案例是观察中国主办国际会议餐饮的典型案例。

Questions 思考题

本次会议在就餐环境方面有何独特之处?
本次会议在餐饮保障方面有何创新之处?

2.4 Case Comparison 案例对比

会议名称	Brisbane's 2014 G20 Leaders' Summit	2014年APEC领导人非正式会议
就餐地点	Queensland's Parliament House	北京水立方
就餐时间	Noon	晚间
宴请原则	4M Principle, Appropriate Principles	4M原则、适量原则
就餐人数	20 Leaders and obeservers	21个经济体领导人及观察员
就餐方式	Barbecue	中餐
食材选择	Vannella buffalo mozzarella with heirloom tomatoes and basil Barbecued new season asparagus, peas, broad beans and goats curd with Mount Zero wild olives Salad with kale, broccoli and avocado with toasted seeds Freshly shucked Moreton Bay rock oysters Cooked Mooloolaba king prawns with lime mayonnaise Moreton Bay bugs, figs, pancetta and fresh bay kebabs with chimichurri Smoked and spiced FlindersIsland butterflied leg of lamb with yoghurt and eggplant Crispy skin Tasmanian ocean trout, avocado, apple, radish and watercress salad	蔬菜、水果、肉类、海鲜等各类食材先抽样检验,再被分类送进各自的加工间接受粗加工、细加工,经过多道手续后,才到大厨手上做成各种美味。 在水果加工间,苹果是逐个被工人手工洗净,再在15摄氏度的环境下切制加工的;在海鲜加工间,虾仁要逐个手工抽掉虾线。 这里的鸡蛋进厨房前,要先被清洗消毒,以防禽流感
菜单制定	Salads Seafood Barbecue Dessert	四菜一汤:上汤响螺、翡翠龙虾、柠汁雪花牛、栗子菜心、北京烤鸭;其后为点心、水果、冰淇淋、咖啡、茶

		酒：长城干红 2006 和长城白干 2011
表演节目	Guitar Show	01. 开场舞 《盛世牡丹》 02. 无伴奏合唱 《青春舞曲》 03. 舞蹈 《鱼跃龙门步步高》 04. 女声独唱 《板蓝花儿开》 05. 芭蕾舞 《天宇流芳》 06. 鼓乐 《云端齐鼓》 07. 男女声二重唱 《今夜无人入睡》 08. 中国戏曲集锦 《姹紫嫣红梨园春》 09. 舞蹈 《千手观音》 10.《同舟共济向明天》

Analysis and Summary 分析概要

根据国际会议餐饮安排的基本内容,案例对比将所选择的中文和英文案例分块进行比较,以突显中外进行国际会议餐饮安排各项具体工作中的异同。

Questions 思考题

1.通过上述两个案例的学习,可否明确国际会议餐饮安排的主要内容?
2.上述两份国际会议餐饮安排在主要内容上有何异同?
3.上述两份国际会议餐饮安排主要内容有何内在联系?

3. Supplementary Reading
拓展阅读

Catering in International Conferences

Catering is a multifaceted segment of the food service industry. There is a niche for all types of catering businesses within the segment of

国际会议餐饮安排 | Catering Arrangement of International Conference

catering. Catering management may be defined as the task of planning, organizing, and controlling. Each activity influences the preparation and delivery of food, beverage, and related services at a competitive, profitable price. These activities work together to meet and exceed the customer's perception of value.

A catering plan serves many purposes. One purpose of a plan is to ensure the caterer's future. A strategic plan is established to guide the entire catering operation over the long term, 3—5 years into the future. It attempts to position the organization on a path of success. A second type of plan, a tactical plan, is specifically created to guide the caterer in a much shorter time frame. A tactical plan creates a forceful focus on each event. Whereas a strategic plan stretches over a long time frame, a tactical plan is specific to the event. A strategic plan requires modification and rejuvenation as forces in the caterer's market shape and reshape it. Since it is over a longer time period, it is much broader and more general in its design. A tactical plan, on the other hand, has a much shorter life span, requires precise detail, and execution.

A plan enables the caterer to establish achievable objectives. Stated objectives flow directly from the mission statement. Objectives are established to serve as benchmarks to measure progress. A caterer can use these benchmarks to compare the actual performance against a predetermined target. This organizational progress can be specified in its strategic plan, or it can be established for each event as measured against a tactical plan. A caterer may create objectives that are beyond the believable accomplishment of the team to stretch the organization to greater levels.

Common organizational objectives may include the measurement of guest satisfaction, attainment of financial goals, human resource development, greater staff productivity levels, increase in market share, and positive organizational growth. For the specific event, tactical objectives might include guest satisfaction, event preparation, familiarity of location, handling guest count, menu item production, preparing the team, and obtaining the required equipment.

Finally, a plan is a blueprint or map. This powerful tool, when properly used by the caterer, keeps everyone in the organization on the right route. A plan helps to minimize unexpected surprises. It attempts to eliminate uncertainties by creating a supportive organizational environment.

资料来源: Stephen B. Shiring, Sr, R. William "Bill" Jardine, Richard J.Mills, Jr, *Catering Management: Ingredients for Success, 3rd Edition,* Delmar,2001.

Blank-filling

Directions: Complete each blank with appropriate words or phrases from the passage.

(　　) belonged to the food service industry. (　　) was regarded as the task of planning, organizing, and controlling. A catering plan serves many purposes. One purpose of a plan is to ensure the caterer's future. A type of plan is specifically created to guide the caterer in a time frame.

Choices

Directions: In this part there are one incomplete sentence. For each sentence there are four choices marked from A to J. Choose the answer that BEST completes the sentence.

What is the basic function for the catering plan?(　　)

A. form an objective

B. reduce the budget

C. avoid a chaos

D. improve the quality of service

国际会议餐饮安排 | Catering Arrangement of International Conference

Exercises
课后练习

1. 阅读下列材料,回答问题。

> **G20 leaders enjoy lavish seafood BBQ**
>
> Instead world leaders tucked into a Queensland delicacy — Moreton Bay bugs — during a seafood cook-up ahead of the official opening of the global leaders' summit on Saturday.
>
> The lunch at Queensland's Parliament House was a fancier version of the traditional Aussie barbecue which generally features burnt — but tasty — sausages.
>
> Brisbane chef Ben O'Donoghue, from Billy Cart Kitchen, also served the heads of state seasonal salads, Mooloolaba king prawns, Moreton Bay bugs, freshly shucked oysters, smoked spiced lamb and Tasmanian ocean trout. The traditional Aussie dessert, pavlova, was served for dessert.
>
>

> Leaders were entertained at the barbecue by renowned classical guitar duo the Grigoryan Brothers. Since their first acclaimed Australian tour in 2002, Slava and Leonard Grigoryan have impressed audiences worldwide with their guitar virtuosity. While best known for their classical repertoire, they also play their own compositions and commissions and take the guitar into genres such as Latin, jazz, folk and contemporary music.

Questions and Answers

Directions: In this part there are three questions. You need to answer the questions based on the words or phrases from the passage.

(1) Did the host of the conference arrange the lunch in a proper way? Please write down your analysis.

(2) If you favor the barbecue as a lunch, what is the specialty at these occasions?

(3) What lesson can we draw from the passage that can be heeded in future international conferences?

国际会议餐饮安排 | Catering Arrangement of International Conference

2.根据下列材料,回答问题。

Breakfast

Conference Breakfast — 8.⁷⁵ per guest
Breakfast Pastries | Choose Three
Includes
Orange Juice, Iced Water
Small World Regular & Decaffeinated Coffee, Hot Tea

Continental Breakfast — 11.²⁵ per guest
Breakfast Pastries | Choose Three
Includes
Sliced Fresh Fruit Platter
Orange Juice, Iced Water
Small World Regular & Decaffeinated Coffee, Hot Tea

Breakfast Buffet 1 — 11.⁷⁵ per guest
10 guest minimum

Fresh Scrambled Eggs
Smoked House Bacon
Assorted Bagels with Cream Cheese
Orange Juice, Iced Water
Small World Regular & Decaffeinated Coffee, Hot Tea

Breakfast Buffet 2 — 17.⁷⁵ per guest
25 guest minimum

Fresh Scrambled Eggs
French Toast with Maple Syrup
Smoked House Bacon, Pork Sausage Links, O'Brien Potatoes
Sliced Fresh Fruit Platter, Strawberry Greek Yogurt
Assorted Bagels with Cream Cheese, Butter, Preserves
Selection of Fruit Juices, Iced Water
Small World Regular & Decaffeinated Coffee, Hot Tea

Mini Fruit Danish
Coffee Crumb Cake
Mini Almond Croissant
Mini Scones
Yogurt Loaf Cakes

Mini Bagels with Cream Cheese
Mini Chocolate Croissant
Mini Muffins
Mini Donuts
Mini Cinnamon Buns

Questions and Answers

Directions: In this part there are three questions. You need to answer the questions based on the words or phrases from the passage.

What are the main types of the breakfast?

What are the limitations for each type?

What is the characteristic of the breakfast?

3. 根据所学的外事礼仪知识，请填写一般国际会议宴请上菜流程。

   第一道菜：

   第二道菜：

   第三道菜：

   第四道菜：

   第五道菜：

   第六道菜：

   第七道菜：

4. 根据所学知识，计算一个拟有200人参加的为期一天的国际会议就餐人数预估表，并给出合理解释。

   7:00早餐人数：　　　　　　理由：

   9:30茶歇人数：　　　　　　理由：

   12:00午餐人数：　　　　　 理由：

   15:00茶歇人数：　　　　　 理由：

   19:00晚餐人数：　　　　　 理由：

5. 观看纪录片《国宴背后的外交风云》，根据所学知识，分析中华人民共和国成立后首次国宴餐饮安排的特色？

Accommodation Arrangement of International Conference
国际会议住宿安排

Overview
内容概览

Accommodation arrangement in international conference is an important part of the pre-meeting work, and the quality of the accommodation has a direct influence on how favorably the participants will acclaim the meeting. The guest room, diet, health, recreation must be considered for accommodation. According to the variety of title, gender, age, and interest, accommodation arrangement must be carefully prepared by the organizer.

会议住宿安排是会议管理工作的一个重要组成部分,工作质量直接影响与会者对会议的评价。住宿要考虑住房、饮食、卫生、娱乐与会议设施的条件能否达到会议的要求。安排参会代表住宿时,要按与会人员的职务、性别、年龄、爱好等进行综合考虑统筹安排。

1. Basic Knowledge
基础知识

1.1 Introduction of Accommodation 住宿基础

Accommodation refers to spending nights, and more often, it refers to short stays outside of one's home. The international conference accommodation focuses more on the foreign guest's accommodations.

For a small international conference, it is very common that the participants find themselves a room to stay. But for a large meeting, accommodation is better fixed up in advance. Conference organizers arrange accommodations in advance in order to facilitate a normal and orderly international convention.

Good rest can help the representatives stay in a good frame of mind. Especially for foreign guests, conference organizers should assist the hotel to create a comfortable atmosphere for the guests and ensure that the guests have a good rest.

A good accommodation environment, and sincere, polite meeting services, can make the participants feel happy, who can attend and participate in the meeting in a good mood, and make it easier to achieve meeting's goals.

Accommodation arrangements are an important part of the work of event organizers, and the service of the accommodation has a direct impact on how positively the participants will evaluate the meeting.

The Meaning of Accommodation 住宿含义

住宿指的是过夜，多指在外暂住。国际会议住宿更多侧重对外宾住宿问题的考虑。

住宿安排有两种情况：一种是自行解决住宿，这种情况适合于小型的国际会议，也是比较理想的安排方式；但对于大型会议来说，统一安排住宿更加合适。会议主办方提前安排好住宿，便于国际会议正常有序地召开。

The Significance of Accommodation in International Meetings 国际会议住宿的意义

（1）Physiological Needs 满足生理需要。

对于参会代表来说，良好的休息有助于保持好的状态。特别是对于那些来自异国他乡的外宾，会务工作人员需要协同酒店保证嘉宾的休息，为嘉宾营造宾至如归的氛围。

（2）Spiritual Needs 满足精神需求。

良好的住宿环境，真诚有礼的会务服务，会让参会人员感到心情舒畅，轻松愉悦，会议更容易达到目标。不仅如此，会议住宿安排还是会议管理工作的一个重要组成部分，工作质量直接影响与会者对会议的评价。

国际会议住宿安排 | Accommodation Arrangement of International Conference

1.2 Factors 住宿安排影响因素

It is expected that most attendees will opt to stay in the venue that hosts the conference, or at a hotel nearby. It is crucial that affordable accommodation options are available within close proximity to the conference venue. It is expected that each "official" conference hotel will provide group discounts for block bookings.

The accommodation affords quiet, secure locations for the attendees' mind and a good night's sleep.

Verify whether the permanent facilities in hotel are complete, whether there will be noise in advance. In general, hotels should be equipped with single rooms, double rooms, standard rooms, business rooms, executive rooms, suites to meet the needs of different participants and staff members.

It is very important to confirm whether the breakfast, lunch and dinner dining place are in the same place in advance, and whether they will be convenient places for guests to go.

The Distance from the Venue, and the Traffic 与会场的距离、交通状况

通常情况下,应尽量安排与会场距离最近、交通最为便捷的酒店或宾馆,最理想的情况是住宿地与会场在同一酒店内。

The Hotel Service Levels and Reception Capacity 酒店服务水平及接待能力

嘉宾入住酒店力求方便、舒适。提前对酒店的接待能力和服务标准进行考察和检验,如是否有过类似的接待外宾的经验,前台人员的英语水平是否合格等等。

Room Types 房间类型

提前考察酒店内的常备设施是否完备,有无噪音问题等等。通常,各类酒店都应配备单人间、双人间、标准间、商务间、行政间、套间等类型的客房,以满足不同与会人员和工作人员的入住需要。

1.3 Process of Accommodation Arrangement 住宿安排流程

Conference planners generally offer delegates different types of accommodation with star-level hotel in the vicinity of the conference venue.

According to the importance of international conferences and the guests who are attending the meeting, the corresponding accommodation was arranged with the special guests, general guests, and staff.

Guest rooms as well as room cards need to be prepared one day before the guests arrive. As there may be many attendees on the meeting day, there are certain requirements for the hotel.

The meeting organizers need to know the timetable for the check-in in advance, the hotel should provide single sign-in desk. In this case, check-in refers to on-site registration, and the guests need to pay a registration fee accordingly.

The event organizers should make the guest accommodation registration form before the arrival of the guests and organize the registration forms in the order of the guest's arrival time. Staff that arranges guest accommodations must work in collaboration with pick-up-personnel and registration personnel. In the process of sending the guests to rooms, staff can explain some requirements of the meeting and accommodation services, etc.

The guests may encounter some unexpected events during their stay, such as injury, forgetting to take the room card, and even losing items, and so on.

The Standards of Accommodation 住宿标准

根据国际会议的重要性及参会嘉宾的职务设定相应的住宿标准，再按特邀嘉宾、一般嘉宾、工作人员安排相应的房间。

Field Investigation 现场调查

嘉宾的房间需要提前准备，要在嘉宾抵达的前一天就将房间办理好，拿到房卡。由于会议当天与会人数众多，多人同时赴会或者转场，都会对酒店的承受能力有一定要求。

Sign in 签到

会议需要在嘉宾入住时签到注册，要求酒店提供单独的签到台。这里的签到指的是现场注册，需要缴纳相应的注册费用。

Hotel Reception 住宿接待

提前做好嘉宾住宿登记表，登记表按嘉宾到达时间先后顺序排列。安排嘉宾住宿的工作人员需要与接机人员和到会注册人员保持畅通的联系，进

国际会议住宿安排 | Accommodation Arrangement of International Conference

行工作协作。在送嘉宾到房间的过程中,可以讲解会议上的一些要求和住宿服务说明等。

Emergency Treatment 紧急情况处理

嘉宾在住宿期间可能会遇到一些意外情况,例如受伤、忘带房卡,甚至丢失物品等。针对这些情况,事先都应该做好安排。

2. Case Study
案例分析

2.1 Case Summary 案例概述

本章选取中外两则案例,通过中英文来展现国际会议住宿安排的异同。第一则案例是国际上举办学术会议时的住宿安排,体现国际会议的一般趋势。第二则案例是中国举办国际会议的组织动员方式,颇具中国办会特色。

2.2 The Automatic Control and Artifical Intelligence Conference

Case Guide-Reading 案例导读

This case is based on the accommodation arrangement of the 2012 Automatic Control and Artificial Intelligence conference. With the full view of the accommodation for this conference, it provides the basic rules and operational standards about the accommodation of the international conference for the reader.

> The IET was formed in March 2006 by the Institution of Electrical Engineers (IEE) and the Institution of Incorporated Engineers (IIE); The IET is one of the world's leading professional societies for the engineering and technology community, with more than 150,000 members in 127 countries and offices in Europe, North America and Asia-Pacific. The IET provides a global knowledge network to facilitate the exchange of ideas and promote the positive role of science, engineering and technology in the world.
>
> The International Conference on Automatic Control and Artificial

Intelligence (ACAI 2012) will be held from March 24th to 26th, 2012 in Xiamen, China.

ACAI 2012 aims to provide a high-level international forum for researchers and engineers to present and discuss recent advances, new techniques and applications in the field of Control Engineering, Manufacturing Engineering and Artificial Intelligence.

Conference Hotel: Fortune Hotel in Xiamen

Image from Fortune Hotel

Fortune Hotel Xiamen offers breathtaking views of Xiamen harbor with elegant five-star hotel environment and is conveniently located on the west of Lujiang River, near the distinctive beautiful Huwei mountain, Yuandang Lake, in the business and executive centre of Xiamen. By car, only 15 minutes from Xiamen Gaoqi International Airport; 10 minutes from Xiamen Railway Station, and 5 minutes from Zhongshan Road shopping district, now a pedestrian street and Gulangyu ferry.

Address: No. 48 Tongyi Road, Xiamen, China

Tel: 86-592-2658888   Fax: 86-592-2659999

Hotel Rooms & Rates:

Standard Room RMB 450/night (about USD 72/night)

Single Room RMB 450/night (about USD 72/night)

How to order the hotel:

Please write email to acaiconf@vip.163.com and reserve the room. You must tell us when will you arrive and who will check in (Authors in China please leave your cell phone number so that we can confirm the information with you).

How to get to the hotel:

1. From Xiamen Binnan Bus Station

You can take 43 bus and get off at International Passenger Travel Port. Then you can see the hotel.

2. From Xiamen Gaoqi International Airport

Take a taxi to Fortune Hotel Xiamen, Tongyi Road, Huli district. Taxi fee is about RMB 24.

3. From Xiamen Railway Station or Wucun Bus Station

You can take 842 bus and get off at International Passenger Travel Port which is near the hotel. You can take a taxi to Fortune Hotel Xiamen, Tongyi Road, Huli district. Taxi fee is about RMB 17.

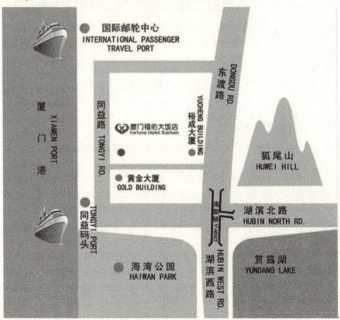

Analysis and Summary 分析概要

This case is selected from ACAI 2012 which fully demonstrates the outline of the accommodation arrangement for international conference. In this case, the room type, the information about the hotel and route from the airport to the hotel are the primary concerns for the organizer. Even though, this conference was held in China, but it still can be regarded as the typical case of the accommodation arrangement in international conference.

Questions 思考题

What is the composition for the accommodation arrangement in this conference? Did the accommodation have any differences from the regular conference in China?

What are the features for the accommodation in this conference?

2.3 2008 中国国际徽商大会

Case Guide-Reading 案例导读

本案例选择了一则中文案例来研究中国主办国际会议时的住宿安排问题。通过学习该案例所提供的会议住宿信息,能够较为全面和直观地掌握中国进行国际会议安排的一般操作方式。

> 中国国际徽商大会是安徽省主办的综合性经贸盛会,意在弘扬徽商精神,展示安徽风貌,促进交流合作,共绘创业蓝图。自2005年创办以来,中国国际徽商大会知名度不断提升,已经成为安徽省规模最大、品位最高、影响最广的对外开放标志性平台。
>
> 2008年5月18—20日,中国国际徽商大会将在我市举办。根据省组委会《2008中国国际徽商大会总体方案》的安排,这次大会参会总人数预计6000人,为做好大会来宾的接待工作,特制定本方案。
>
> 一、来宾类型
>   1. 党和国家领导人
>   2. 国家部委(办、局)领导
>   3. 省领导

国际会议住宿安排 | Accommodation Arrangement of International Conference

4. 省直单位领导
5. 世界500强及其他大企业高管理人员
6. 国内大企业领导
7. 境外行业商会及其他机构高层人员
8. 联合国及国际组织高层人员
9. 皖籍和在皖工作过的领导、知名人士及企业家
10. 国外结好城市团组
11. 国外驻华大使、总领事
12. 各地徽商社团及著名徽商
13. 十六个兄弟市领导
14. 新闻记者
15. 演职人员
16. 我市邀请的客商

二、接待要求及分工

根据总体方案要求,由我市承担大会来宾的接待工作,实行对口接待和谁邀请谁接待的原则。

1. 市外办根据省外办的要求,做好外宾的接待工作。由夏永根、程华荣负责统筹。

2. 市接待办根据省接待办的要求,做好国家领导人和省部级领导的生活服务安排。由吴民负责统筹。

3. 市直有关单位派员做好国家部委(办、局)的领导和省直领导的对口接待工作。由黄宏建负责统筹。

4. 市各大办公厅派员做好省领导的对口接待工作。由吴民负责统筹。

5. 市直各有关单位派员做好十六个兄弟市来宾的接待工作。由程顺生、王勇负责统筹。

三、酒店安排

(一)房源基本情况

我市64家二星级以上酒店。其中大会可用的中心城区23家、徽州区2家、歙县7家、休宁2家、汤口2家,共36家。现在宝莱半岛、徽商国际、豪生、金融山庄、莫泰168、东方假日、胡开文、宝利风尚等酒店都

57

已列入徽商大会接待酒店范围。加上今年3月份将要开业的茶博园等酒店,中心城区及附近区县目前可用酒店近50家用房预计可达5300多间。客房总数可基本满足来宾的需求。

(二)入住初步安排

省里初步排定:

(1)国家领导人、国家部委领导、省领导、部分省直单位领导以及部分重要客商安排在高尔夫酒店。

(2)省里邀请的其他重要客商分别安排在国大、华山、云松、徽商国际大酒店。

(3)新闻中心预计设在梅地亚酒店,记者全部安排在该酒店。

(三)房源摸排

5月中旬是我市旅游旺季的高峰期,为了保证全部来宾都能顺利入住酒店,必须做好房源控制工作。进一步摸排可住酒店,掌握更为准确的、足够数量的酒店和客房总数并形成相对完整的一览表。

(四)房源控制

2月中旬以前以市徽商大会筹委会的名义向中心城区及周边地区三星级以及相当于三星级的各类酒店发函帮助各地来宾控房,控房总数在6000人的入住规模。另外宝莱半岛(一部分)、胡开文、宝利风尚等三个酒店为市筹委会控房,用于我市邀请客商住宿和应急所需。各酒店必须以徽商大会为主,根据筹备组的要求提供足够数量的客房、合理的价格(费用自负的客人可直接与酒店商定价格)及优质服务。

(五)订房原则

及时与省里和各市对接,尽快确定各类来宾入住的酒店。近期以省大会组委会(我市代拟通知并经省里同意)的名义向各市发出通知:一是3月10日以前请各市在我市自行订房(我们提供详实的房源一览表,并及时掌握各市订房情况);二是3月10日后各市用房凡未确定的,由省大会组委会分配客房并请各市向指定酒店打入定金;三是3月底以前凡未向指定酒店打入定金的,大会期间所需住房由其自行解决。

Analysis and Summary 分析概要

该案例选取一个中文国际会议作为样本,全面展现了中国举办国际会议

国际会议住宿安排 | Accommodation Arrangement of International Conference

的住宿安排全貌。由该案例可以看出,国内有关单位在进行国际会议住宿安排时较为重视来宾类型、房间安排这几方面的内容。该案例体现出中国有关方面在举办国际会议住宿安排的一般原则。

Questions 思考题

1. 在该案例中,国际会议的住宿安排由哪几部分构成?这样的构成与国外举办国际会议的住宿安排有何差异?
2. 在该案例中,国际会议的住宿安排有何特性?这样的住宿安排与一般国内国际会议的住宿安排有何差异?

2.4 Case Comparison 案例对比

会议名称	2008中国国际徽商大会	The International Conference on Automatic Control and Artifical Intelligence (ACAI 2012)
住宿星级	64家二星级以上酒店,根据客人级别分配酒店	five star
住宿地点	中心城区23家;徽州区2家;歙县7家;休宁2家;汤口2家;宝莱半岛、徽商国际、豪生、金融山庄、莫泰168、东方假日、胡开文、宝利风尚等酒店都已列入徽商大会接待酒店范围、茶博园等酒店 中心城区及附近区县目前可用酒店近50家用房预计可达5300多间	No. 48 Tongyi Road, Xiamen, near venue
住宿位置	中心城区及附近	Fortune Hotel Xiamen offers breathtaking views of Xiamen harbor with elegant five-star hotel environment and is conveniently located on the west of Lujiang

59

		River, near the distinctive beautiful Huwei mountain, Yuandang Lake, in the business and executive centre of Xiamen
房间类型	套房、标间	Standard Room RMB Single Room RMB 450/night
就餐场所	酒店餐厅	Hotel

Analysis and Summary 分析概要

根据国际会议住宿安排的基本内容,案例对比将所选择的中文和英文案例分块进行比较,以突显中外进行国际会议住宿安排各项具体工作中的异同。

Questions 思考题

1. 通过上述两个案例的学习,可否明确国际会议住宿安排的主要内容?
2. 上述两份国际会议住宿安排在主要内容上有何异同?
3. 上述两份国际会议住宿安排主要内容有何内在联系?

3. Supplementary Reading
拓展阅读

3.1 2012 London Olympics

> The 2012 Summer Olympics, formally the Games of the XXX Olympiad and commonly known as London 2012, was a major international multi-sport event celebrated in the tradition of the Olympic Games, as governed by the International Olympic Committee (IOC). It took place in London, United Kingdom and to a lesser extent across the country from 25 July to 12 August 2012. The first event, the group stage in women's football began on 25 July at the Millennium Stadium in Cardiff, followed by the opening ceremonies on 27 July. More than 10,000 athletes from 204 National Olympic Committees (NOCs) participated.

国际会议住宿安排 | Accommodation Arrangement of International Conference

Following a bid headed by former Olympic champion Sebastian Coe and then-Mayor of London Ken Livingstone, London was selected as the host city on 6 July 2005 during the 117th IOC Session in Singapore, defeating bids from Moscow, New York City, Madrid and Paris. London was the first city to host the modern Olympic Games three times, having previously done so in 1908 and in 1948.

Construction for the Games involved considerable redevelopment, with an emphasis on sustainability. The main focus was a new 200-hectare (490-acre) Olympic Park, constructed on a former industrial site at Stratford, East London. The Games also made use of venues that already existed before the bid.

The Games received widespread acclaim for their organization, with the volunteers, the British military and public enthusiasm praised particularly highly. The opening ceremony, directed by Danny Boyle, received widespread acclaim throughout the world, particular praise from the British public and a minority of widely ranging criticisms from some social media sites. During the Games, Michael Phelps became the most decorated Olympic athlete of all time, winning his 22nd medal. Saudi Arabia, Qatar and Brunei entered female athletes for the first time, so that every currently eligible country has sent a female competitor to at least one Olympic Games. Women's boxing was included for the first time, thus the Games became the first at which every sport had female competitors.

These were the final Olympic Games under the IOC presidency of Jacques Rogge.

Modules	Problems	Contents
Facilities	Small Bed	The bed is only 5 feet and 8 inches, which is small for most athletes.
Rooms	Multi-share Room rather than Standard Room or Single Room	Because of the Financial Crisis, Organizing Committee reduced the amount of rooms from 4000 to 2800, which caused the athletes have to be accustomed with Multishare Rooms.

True or False

Directions: Complete each blank with appropriate words or phrases from the passage.

London was the first city to host the modern Olympic Games (   ), having previously done so in 1908 and in 1948.

Questions

Directions: In this part there is one question. You need to answer the question based on the words or phrases from the passage.

What is(are) the problem(s) in the 2012 Summer Olympics?

3.2 雁栖湖

2014年APEC领导人非正式会议将在北京雁栖湖举行。它主要包括一座国际会议中心、一座精品酒店和12栋贵宾别墅。

雁栖湖位于北京市东北部、怀柔新城以北的雁栖镇,风景秀美,生态和谐。它的环境、建筑、能源等方面,始终以"低碳、自然生态、节能环保"为理念和标准,综合利用70余项世界领先的生态环保技术,清洁能源使用率、污水处理率、生活垃圾无害化处理率等均达到100%,将雁栖湖建设成为低碳节能项目的典范。

北京将继续坚持首善标准,精益求精地做好各项工作,为与会嘉宾提供周到细致的服务,全力打造"北京服务"品牌。

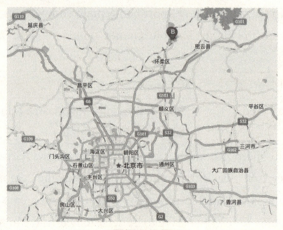

雁栖湖位置

国际会议住宿安排 | Accommodation Arrangement of International Conference

雁栖湖一景

　　北京雁栖湖建设秉承"低碳环保、科技创新"的理念，应用70余项世界领先的生态环保技术，将使清洁能源使用率、太阳能生活热水覆盖率、生活垃圾无害化处理率、餐厨垃圾处理资源化利用率、污水处理率、水土保持方案实施率和水体生态护岸实施率均达到100%。

雁栖湖高空俯瞰图

问答

1. 结合图文信息,分析雁西湖作为会议住宿地点的自然条件优势?

2. 结合材料,分析本次会议住宿地点的选址建设后,对当地的环境保护的影响?

Exercises
课后练习

1. 阅读下面的材料,回答问题。

19th International Conference on Electron Dynamics in Semiconductors, Optoelectronics and Nanostructures EDISON'19

June 29 — July 2, 2015; Salamanca, Spain

Accommodation Form

Please download, complete electronically this form and save it (in PDF format, if you have Acrobat Professional or in PS format with Acrobat Reader) and e-mail it to edison19@alacarta.es.

Rates and availability will not be guaranteed for reservations made after May 17, 2015.

Surname:_____ First Name:_____ Title/Position:_____
Organization:_____
Address:_____
City:_____ State/Province:_____ Country:_____ Postal Code:_____
Phone:_____ Fax:_____ E-mail:_____

国际会议住宿安排 | Accommodation Arrangement of International Conference

First name and family name of the ACCOMPANYING PERSONS
_____
_____

Arrival: _____ 2015   Departure: _____ 2015

1st Choice_____
2nd Choice_____

To secure your accommodation you must provide a credit card number. Your credit card details will be forward to the hotel prior to your arrival to secure your reservation, but they will only be processed in the event of late cancellation or non arrival.

Credit Card Type: _____ Card Number:_____ Expiration Date:_____
Name as shown on card :_____

CANCELLATION: Cancellations must be received in writing before June 10, 2015, after this date a fee equivalent to the price of a room for one night will be charged.
PAYMENT: Payment should be made directly at the hotel during your stay.

Chart-filling

Directions: If you are the participants from China, please fill out the blanks with appropriate words or phrases.

65

Questions and Answers

Directions: In this part there is one question. You need to answer the question based on the knowledge you get from this chapter.

What are the general rules for the accommodation form in the international conference you can get from this case?

2.阅读材料,回答问题

Gaddafi Can't Find Place to Sleep in New York

Libyan leader Muammar Gaddafi looks for place to stay while in city for UN General Assembly. After being turned down by number of hotels, he is forced to make do with Manhattan home of Libyan ambassador to UN.

Life is hard in the United States for a number of world leaders. Libyan Muammar Gaddafi, who planned on sleeping in a tent encampment in a posh New Jersey neighborhood until the plan was thwarted by New Jersey's governor, was forced to search for lodgings in Manhattan.

Fox News reported Tuesday that a number of New York hotels refused to host Gaddafi because of his involvement in the attack on the Pan Am flight over Lockerbie, Scotland in 1988. Ultimately, the leader decided to forego finding a hotel in face of the harsh criticism that surfaced regarding his booking in the Pierre Hotel, and decided instead to stay at the home of the Libyan ambassador to the UN.

Of course, the US will not actually go ahead with such a move. Instead, Gaddafi will actually be invited to speak at the UN General Assembly Wednesday following the address of US President Barack Obama.

The US is committed to allow representatives of each of the 192 UN member states to come to New York for the General Assembly and be allowed to move freely within a 40 kilometers (about 25 miles) radius from the UN headquarters.

国际会议住宿安排 | Accommodation Arrangement of International Conference

Analysis

Based on this case, why did the American hotels turn their back to Muammar Gaddafi?

Scenario Decision

Suppose you are the decision-maker for the conference, how can you avoid the dilemma in this case? Why did the hotel refuse to accept some guests?

3.阅读材料,回答问题

> 金砖国家学术论坛、金砖国家工商论坛先于金砖国家领导人峰会召开,会议成果将成为领导人峰会的重要议题,对于推动金砖国家合作意义重大。
>
> 2014年金砖国家智库理事会第三次会议暨第六次金砖国家学术论坛在巴西里约热内卢召开,主办方安排与会者入住 Windsor Excelsior Hotel。
>
> Tradition and modernity in a single place. This is the Windsor Excelsior Hotel, in Copacabana, one of the main postcards of Rio de Janeiro. Guests just cross the street to swim in the green waters of the sea of Copacabana, without worrying about chairs and towels. The hotel provides everything as a courtesy. Then, if you want to go out for a while and experience the beauty of Rio de Janeiro, the Windsor Excelsior is a key point, providing easy access to major points of the city.
>
> If you search quality and good service, the Windsor Excelsior Hotel is an excellent choice. All the catering team is ready to welcome you friendly and efficiently.
>
> The view from the rooms is a special show — no comments. Not to mention the breakfast included in the rate, which is an attack on any diet. Simply irresistible.
>
> Whether in Copacabana, come to the Windsor Excelsior Hotel and experience the best of Rio de Janeiro.

The location of Windsor Excelsior Hotel

Near Windsor Excelsior are some of the main attractions of Rio de Janeiro. Those are Ristorante Alloro, Sá Restaurant, Catete Palace & Republic Museum, Rio de Janeiro Municipal Theater, Botanical Garden, Maracanã Soccer Stadium, MAM — Modern Art Museum, National History Museum, Copacabana Beach, Trade at Copacabana street, Copacabana Fort, Leme Fort, Ipanema, Rio Sul Shopping Center, Botafogopraia Shopping.

Images from the homepage of the hotel

国际会议住宿安排 | Accommodation Arrangement of International Conference

(1) 根据材料,试分析主办方对于住宿安排的别出心裁。

(2) 这样的安排对于本次会议有何意义?

(3) 本案例中的住宿安排对于国际会议住宿安排有何启示?

4. 阅读以下国际会议主办方提供的信息,回答问题。

参会地点

　　第八届固体废物管理与技术国际会议于2013年10月23日上午8:30在上海浦东华美达大酒店开幕,会议持续至10月25日。

　　全新的上海浦东华美达大酒店坐落于浦东会展商务和高科技园区中心地带,交通便利。

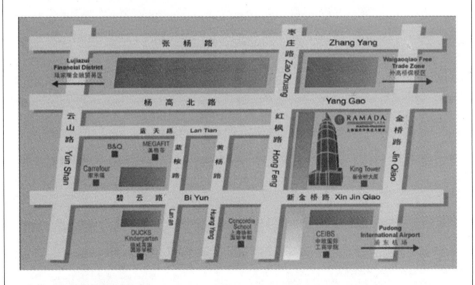

会议地址及联系电话

　　地址:上海浦东新区新金桥路18号　　电话:021-5055×××

乘车路线
1. 浦东机场到会场

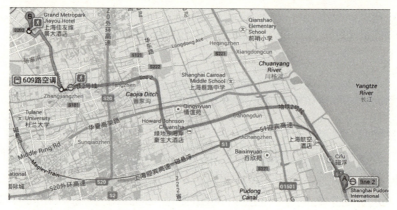

2. 虹桥机场到会场

3. 虹桥火车站到会场

国际会议住宿安排 | Accommodation Arrangement of International Conference

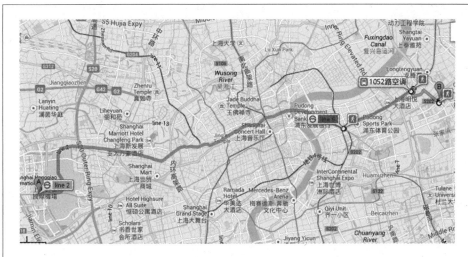

图片来自会议公告

组委会推荐的宾馆信息

大会组委会为参会代表推荐以下宾馆,请代表们参考宾馆信息自行预定房间。由于会议期间附近宾馆房源紧张,建议您及早预订。已经在会议系统中办理宾馆预定的可直接前往预订宾馆办理入住。入住宾馆时报会议名称即可享受协议价格。

酒店名称	地址	电话	房型	门市价格	优惠价格	房间数
上海碧云宾乐雅高级服务公寓	上海市碧云路1199弄	021-2060888	一房一厅(64-78m2)	900	700含早	100
			二房二厅(130-166m2)	1500	1100含早	100
上海浦东华美达大酒店	上海浦东新金桥路18号	021-50554666	大床房	-	760单早	50
			标间双床	-	920双早	35
汉庭新金桥路店	新金桥路230号17-6(近金藏路)	021-60897366	双床房	284	263	15
			高级大床	246	228	20
汉庭碧云店	黄杨路221号	021-31271388	双床房	246	246	25
			高级大床	284	228	30
如家(杨高中路店)	杨高中路758号(苏先生旁)	021-50706006	大床房	259	259含早	20
			标准双床	259	259含早	20

(1) 根据会议主办方所提供的信息,试分析外地和国内代表前来参会在交通方面可能产生的问题。

(2) 根据会议主办方所提供的信息,请分析主办方的住宿安排是否合理,并给出与会者的解释。

(3) 结合材料,请分析在大城市繁华中心举办国际会议,主办方在住宿安排方面应注意哪些事项。

Traffic Arrangement of International Conference
国际会议交通安排

Overview 内容概览

Reasonable and orderly traffic arrangement is an important condition for meeting under normal circumstances. Transport arrangements take a very important part in an international conference. This chapter gives a brief introduction to the international conference traffic arrangements and relevant theoretical knowledge through selected case studies, and this would allow students deepen their understanding about the traffic arrangement in the international conference.

合理有序的交通安排是会议得以正常召开的重要条件。国际会议交通安排事关重大,是国际会议筹划中很重要的一部分。本章的基础知识部分简要介绍了国际会议交通安排相关的理论知识,通过精选案例的学习,完成实践操作的内容,进而加深对知识的了解,并巩固所学的知识。合理、良好的交通安排能保证与会者准时参会及会议顺利进行,有助于保证会议质量。国际会议交通安排指的是做好会议期间的交通保障工作,其主要内容是建立用车制度,根据会议的整体安排制订详细的用车计划并及时调度以满足会议需求,同时要做好宾客的迎送服务工作。

1. Basic Knowledge
基础知识

1.1 Transport Security of International Conference 国际会议交通保障

Transportation, in ancient time, referred to staggered communication. Today, it refers to a variety of transports and telecommunications in general. It indicates the exchange of all traffic flow through transport such as trains, automobiles, motorcycles, ships, aircraft, etc.

International conference transport arrangements can guarantee good working transport during the meeting. The organizer should establish a rental car system, to develop a detailed plan based on the overall arrangements for the meeting and the conference scheduled in time, and welcome and bid farewell the guests as well.

Traffic 交通

交通，古义指交错相通，今义指各种运输和邮电事业的总称。交通是指所有通过火车、汽车、摩托车、轮船、飞机等工具，或仅靠人力进行的人流、客流和货流的交流运输。

Traffic Security of International Conference 国际会议交通保障

国际会议交通保障指的是做好会议期间的交通保障工作。会议交通保障工作的主要内容是建立用车制度，根据会议的整体安排制订详细的用车计划并及时调度以满足会议需求，同时要做好宾客的迎送服务工作。

1.2 International Conference Traffic Arrangement 国际会议交通安排

It is important to consider the distance among the airport, venue and the hotel before the most convenient way was chosen. For group activities, organizers need an adjustable vehicle scheduling, just ensure that the participants take cars smoothly.

In order to develop the most accurate schedule and try to avoid road congestion, Organizers should consult with local experienced drivers about the road congestion during each period of the day in advance,.

国际会议交通安排 | Traffic Arrangement of International Conference

Vehicle Selecting 交通工具的选择

根据嘉宾住宿场所与机场的距离,以及会议举办地点和沿途路线来选择方便快捷的用车方式。因为车辆人员众多,必须加强车辆调度、用车检查和驾驶员的管理,保证与会人员按号入座,有序乘车。

Arrangement of Transport Schedule 交通时间的安排

提前与当地经验丰富的司机咨询会议举办当天各时段的道路拥堵情况,尽量制定出最为准确的时间表,尽量避免因道路堵塞而影响行程,必要时还要采取相应的交通管制。

1.3 Pick-up Process 接机流程

A clear and simple plan should ensure that all staffs know when and where to go, and what to do. A pick-up list should include the names and contact information of guests, flight information, airport staff names, and contact information (guests that arrive at the adjacent time should be carpooled together), vehicle information, etc.

In order to ensure driver and vehicle in place on time, it is necessary to contact the driver half an hour before departure. At the same time, organizers should check the vehicle to ensure that it meets the requirements. According to the road and weather conditions, it is important for the organizer to make corresponding adjustments to the driver to pick-up.

Pick-up cards generally have two functions: one is to demonstrate the conference name, and the other is to match with the guests. To ensure that guests can find staff, an airport pick-up card is very important.

Pick-up staffs should check flight information, confirm the exit that guests may come from, and make themselves available in advance. Pick-up staffs should patiently wait for the guests in easily visible places in order to help guests to find them easily.

After receiving the guests, pick-up staffs should lead the guests to the cars and notify the staff who are responsible for the registration and the living quarters of the guests, to make sure that everything is prepared in advance.

For the participants take other modes of transport, the pick-up task follows the similar procedure.

Making Detailed Pick-up Table 制作详细的接机表

一份明晰简洁的接机表让所有工作人员知道自己应该在什么时间,到哪儿去,去做什么。一份接机表应包括嘉宾的名字及联系方式,航班信息,接机人员的名字及联系方式,相邻时间到达的嘉宾凑一起接,车辆信息等。

Contact the Driver 联系司机

在出发半小时前与司机联系,以保证司机与车辆能按时就位。同时应该检查车辆是否符合要求。与司机保持联系,根据路况、天气状况做出相应的调整。

Pick Carry Cards 携带接机牌

接机牌一般有两种形式,一种是展示会议名称的,另一种是标有嘉宾名字的。为保证嘉宾能找到工作人员,携带接机牌很重要。

Check Flight Information Again 再次查询航班信息

查询航班信息,确认嘉宾会从某个出口出来,提前在可能会出现的出口做好接待准备。

Waiting and Receive Guests 等待并接待嘉宾

耐心等待嘉宾,最好在比较明显的地方,便于嘉宾寻找,以免出现嘉宾走失的情况。

Leading the Guests to Take the Car 引领嘉宾上车

接到嘉宾后,引导嘉宾上车,及时通知办理注册与嘉宾入住的人员,方便其提前做好准备。

对于搭乘其他交通工具来参会的代表,交通保障工作流程类似接机流程。

1.4 The Transport Costs of International Conference 国际会议交通费用

Travel costs include the cost of transportation such as flights, railways, highways, passenger ships, as well as the transportation costs from destination stations, airports, and wharves to the accommodation.

Conference costs include the costs from flight, rail, road, ferry and the accommodation to the airport, railway stations, and ports transport. When an accident happens, the relevant authorities should be notified as soon as possible,

国际会议交通安排 | Traffic Arrangement of International Conference

Insurance must be notified immediately, no more than 24 hours after the accident.

Transportation Costs to the Conference 出发地至会务地的交通费用

出发地至会务地的交通费用包括航班、铁路、公路、客轮,以及目的地车站、机场、码头至住宿地的交通费用。

Transport Costs during the Meeting 会议期间交通费用

会议期间交通费用主要是会务地交通费用,包括住宿地至会所的交通、会所到餐饮地点的交通、会所到商务交际场地的交通、商务考察交通以及其他与会人员可能使用的预定交通。

Farewell and Return Transportation 欢送及返程交通

欢送交通及返程交通包括航班、铁路、公路、客轮及住宿地至机场、车站、港口交通费用。一旦发生事故,应尽快通知相关部门,一定要有交警的事故判定书或是安委会的证明。这两样是保险理赔所必需的证明。保险一定要在第一时间通知,最迟不能超过24小时。

2. Case Study 案例分析

2.1 Case Summary 案例概述

本章选择中外两则案例来展现国际会议交通安排的异同。第一则英文案例是国际会议中对交通管制的通行做法。第二则中文案例反映了地方政府在举办国际会议时的交通安排的通则。

2.2 2010 G8 Muskoka Summit

Case Guide-Reading 案例导读

This case is based on the traffic arrangement of G8 Summit. With the demonstration of the traffic plan for this conference, it provides the basic rules and operational standards about the traffic arrangement of the international conference for the reader.

The 36th G8 Summit was held in Huntsville, Ontario, Canada, on June 25—26, 2010. In this year's meeting, the G8 leaders agreed in reaffirming the group's essential and continuing role in international affairs and "assertions of new-found relevance." The form and function of the G8 was reevaluated as the G20 summits evolved into the premier forum for discussing, planning and monitoring international economic cooperation.

Agenda

Traditionally, the host country of the G8 Summit sets the agenda for negotiations, which take place primarily amongst multi-national civil servants in the weeks before the summit itself, leading to a joint declaration which all countries can agree to sign.

In early June, Harper was more specific. Canada wanted to focus on the economy, with emphasis placed on reforming the financial sector, and finding European support for plans to return to fiscal stability.

The summit was intended as a venue for resolving differences among its members. As a practical matter, the summit was also conceived as an opportunity for its members to give each other mutual encouragement in the face of difficult economic decisions.

Core G8 members

Canada	France	Germany
Italy	Japan	Russia
United Kingdom	United States	

Traffic Restrictions

Before, during and after the G8 Summit, there will be a significant number of police officers and increased security in the Huntsville and Muskoka regions. There will be a total marine exclusion zone on Fairy and Peninsula lakes as well as on the canal that links them. This will apply to all motorized vessels and non-motorized craft.

国际会议交通安排 | Traffic Arrangement of International Conference

Harp Lake Road and Williamsport Road will be accessible only to people living on these roads or those visiting them. No detour or through traffic will be allowed. Limberlost Road, Highway 60 east of Hidden Valley Road.

Residents living on these roads or travelling to and from Limberlost Road and Highway 60 east of the easternmost security gate will have to travel east on Highway 60 and south on Muskoka Road #9 (South Portage Road), to access the southern detour route to go to Huntsville. Through-traffic: heavy commercial vehicles and cars will be rerouted to Highways 11, 35 and 118 (in green).

Cars traveling through the area, semi-trailer trucks, buses and other heavy vehicles should use Highway 118 to bypass the restrictions on Highway 60.Those coming from the South will get off Highway 11 at Highway 118 and proceed to Highway 35 and then Highway 60, east of the restricted area.Those coming from the North will have to go past Huntsville to Highway 118. Local commercial traffic, delivery trucks and heavy vehicles (in blue).

Delivery trucks and other heavy vehicles from the local Huntsville area will be able to use the following alternate routes to bypass the restricted section of Highway 60: Muskoka roads 3, 9 (South Portage Road) and 10 (Britannia Road) and Brunel Road. Car-only roads (in orange).

For safety reasons, certain area roads have been identified as being able to bear cars only. They include: White House and West Brown roads, in addition to Muskoka Road 10 (Britannia Road), Restricted access (in red), A section of Highway 60 and local roads, including Muskoka Road 23 (Canal Road), closest to Deerhurst Resort will not be accessible except to those with proper accreditations: emergency services workers, residents and employees of local businesses.

Analysis and Summary 分析概要

This case is selected from 2010 G8 Muskoka Summit which fully expresses the overall performance of the traffic arrangement for this conference. In this case, the traffic plan, traffic restrictions and areas are the primary concerns for the organizer. The schedule can be recognized as the typical case of the traffic arrangement in international conference.

Questions 思考题

1. What are the traffic restrictions for this conference?
2. Compared with the traffic restrictions during a conference at home, what are the features for that of this conference?

2.3 2008 徽商大会交通保障方案

Case Guide-Reading 案例导读

本案例选取一则中文案例来研究国际会议交通安排。通过详细展现该国际会议的交通安排,读者可以通过详实的资料来掌握国内国际会议交通安排的基本规划和操作流程。

> 2008 中国国际徽商大会将于 2008 年 5 月 18 日至 20 日在黄山市(屯溪)召开,为保障大会期间辖区内道路畅通及交通安全,根据《2008 中国国际徽商大会黄山市总体方案》的要求,特制定本方案。
>
> 一、保障范围
> 徽商大会期间市内公路(含景区景点旅游公路)交通运输保障、交通安全保障。公路安全畅通保障、水上交通安全应急保障、航空运输保障、铁路运输保障、城市公交保障。
>
> 二、组织机构
> 在市筹委会领导下,交通协调组下设办公室和公路运输保障、交通安全保障、公路畅通保障、水上交通安全应急保障、航空运输保障、铁路运输保障、城市公交保障等 7 个工作小组,各小组下设组长,成立相应机构,制定子预案。办公室设在市交通局。

国际会议交通安排 | Traffic Arrangement of International Conference

三、保障要求

（一）市内公路交通运输保障

 1. 运力组织

  ……

 2. 保障措施

  ……

 3. 应急队伍保障

  ……

（二）交通安全保障

由市交警支队负责徽商大会期间交通管理，会议车辆的道路交通运输安全；临时通道的封闭、开启；重要车辆的引导；临时交通管制等。

（三）公路畅通保障

 1. 保障范围

  ……

 2. 保障目标

  ……

 3. 保障措施

 （1）成立公路安全畅通保障组织

  市公路局成立"2008中国国际徽商大会"公路安全畅通保障领导小组，组长由市公路局负责人担任，刘××、陈××、方××同志担任副组长，成员有：蔡××、姚××……

  市路桥工程处组建桥梁应急抢险中队，市机械化筑路处组建道路应急抢险中队，各区县分局分别成立公路应急抢险分队，中队长、分队长由各单位负责人担任，实行单位领导负责制。

  ……

 （2）全市应急抢险机械、人员配备

  ……

 （3）预防与应急准备

  ……

（4）应急处理
　　　　……
（四）水上交通安全应急保障
　　1. 应急防范范围
　　　　……
　　2. 应急防范对象
　　　　……
　　3. 应急防范措施
　　　　……
　　4. 应急队伍设施
　　（1）应急队伍保障
　　　　市地方海事局成立"2008中国国际徽商大会"屯溪中心城区水上交通安全应急领导小组及现场监管值勤小组。
　　　　应急领导小组组长：方××。副组长：曹××。成员：……
　　　　设立1个指挥组和3个现场值勤组：
　　　　指挥组：方××（组长）……，负责指挥值勤（应急）小组各项工作。
　　　　第1值勤组：曹××（组长）……，负责协调现场值勤和屯溪中心城区水域内通航秩序保障管理。
　　　　第2值勤组：姚××（组长）……，负责屯溪中心城区世纪广场码头现场监管。
　　　　第3值勤组：胡××（组长）……，负责屯溪中心城区三马路口码头现场监管。
　　　　必要时可从歙县处、黄山区处抽调海事执法人员协助参与值勤监管。
　　（2）应急设施保障
　　　　……
　　5. 险情处置程序。
　　　　……

国际会议交通安排 | Traffic Arrangement of International Conference

> （五）航空运输保障
>   由口岸办、黄山机场负责，做好境外航班包机的申报，负责机场航班的安全起降和突发事件的处理。
> （六）徽商大会期间铁路运输保障
>   由铁路黄山站负责，负责铁路安全输送境内外客商。
> （七）徽商大会期间城市公交保障
>   由市建委、公交公司负责，做好徽商大会期间公交车辆运行，保障客商市内通行。

Analysis and Summary 分析概要

　　该案例选取一个中文国际会议作为样本，全面展现了国内举办国际会议的交通安排全貌。由该案例可以看出，国内有关单位进行国际会议住宿安排时较为重视交通保障领导和组织工作，由具体机构和人员负责相关事宜，强调有关方面的广泛动员和联动。该案例是国内有关单位举办国际会议时交通保障的通行做法，具有典型代表性。

Questions 思考题

1. 在该案例中，国际会议的交通保障有哪些具体举措？
2. 在该案例中，国际会议的交通保障与一般国外国际会议的交通保障有何差异？

2.4 Case Comparison 案例对比

会议名称	2008中国国际徽商大会	2010 G8 Muskoka Summit
交通范围	黄山市（屯溪）	Huntsville（Canada）
组织机构	在市筹委会领导下，交通协调组下设办公室和公路运输保障、交通安全保障、公路畅通保障、水上交通安全应急保障、航空运输保障、铁路运输保障、城市公交保障等7个工作小组。各小组应成立相应机构，制定子预案。办公室设在市交通局	Local police officers

保障要求	市内公路交通运输保障 交通安全保障 公路畅通保障 水上交通安全应急保障	Residential access only (in pink) Limberlost Road, Highway 60 east of Hidden Valley Road Through-traffic: heavy commercial vehicles and cars will be rerouted to Highways 11, 35 and 118 (in green) Local commercial traffic, delivery trucks and heavy vehicles (in blue) Car-only roads (in orange) Restricted access (in red)

Analysis and Summary 分析概要

根据国际会议交通安排的基本内容,案例对比将所选择的中文和英文案例分块进行比较,以突显中外进行国际会议交通安排各项具体工作中的异同。

Questions 思考题

1. 通过上述两个案例的学习,可否明确国际会议交通安排的主要内容?
2. 上述两份国际会议交通安排在主要内容上有何异同?
3. 上述两份国际会议交通安排主要内容有何内在联系?

国际会议交通安排 | Traffic Arrangement of International Conference

3. Supplementary Reading
拓展阅读

3.1 2009 Thailand ASEAN Summit

The ASEAN Summit is an annual meeting held by the member of the Association of Southeast Asian Nations in relation to economic, and cultural development of Southeast Asian countries.

The league of ASEAN is currently connected with other countries who aimed to participate on the missions and visions of the league. Apparently, the league is conducting an annual meeting with other countries in an organization collectively known as the ASEAN dialogue partners. ASEAN +3 adds China, Japan and South Korea. The formal summit is held in three days. The usual itinerary are as follows:

ASEAN leaders hold an internal organization meeting.

ASEAN leaders hold a conference together with foreign ministers of the ASEAN Regional Forum.

Leaders of 3 ASEAN Dialogue Partners (also known as ASEAN+3) namely China, Japan and South Korea hold a meeting with the ASEAN leaders.

And a separate meeting is set for leaders of 2 ASEAN Dialogue Partners (also known as ASEAN + CER) namely Australia and New Zealand.

The 15th Asean Summit was held from 23—25 October 2009 in HuaHin, Cha Am, Thailand. It involved the Leaders from Asean league of Nations together with their dialogue partners from People's Republic of China, Japan, South Korea, India, Australia and New Zealand.

Modules	Problems	Contents
Organizers	Chaos	Protesters blocked Sukhumvit 71 and a Vibhavadi highway — Suthisarn Road junction. Protesters retreated from the Democracy Monument to the main rally site in front of Government House. Protesters clashed with Police, and marched to ASEAN Summit Venue.
Ensurance	Out of Position	Protesters occupied the airport and the airport was shuttled.

Blank-filling

Directions: Complete the brackets with appropriate words or phrases from the passage.

(   ) is the abbreviation of the Association of Southeast Asian Nations.

Questions

Directions: In this part there is one question. You need to answer the question based on the words or phrases from the passage.

What are the common activities during the ASEAN Summit?

Summarization

Directions: In this part there is one question, there are four choices marked from A to D. Choose the ONE answer that best completes the sentence.

One of the most challengeable issues for the traffic organization in ASEAN Summit is (   ).

A. airport   B. car   C. bus   D. bicycle

3.2 2015亚欧商品贸易博览会交通保障方案

2015亚欧商品贸易博览会(以下简称"商博会")将于8月12日至16日在新疆国际会展中心(以下简称"会展中心")举行。

为确保论坛及商博会期间会展中心场馆及人员安全,在会展中心

国际会议交通安排 ｜ Traffic Arrangement of International Conference

周边设置交通管制区域(点)。

管制区域:红光山路与会展经六路路口至红光山路与米东南路路口;会展大道与龙盛街路口至会展大道与会展北路路口。上述区域除持有博览会通行证的车辆、特种车辆、摆渡公交车和具有博览会专用车辆标志的出租车外,其他车辆禁止通行。

管制点:在红光山路与会展经六路路口(简称"东管制点")、会展大道与龙盛街路口(简称"南管制点")、红光山路与米东南路路口(简称"西管制点")、会展大道与会展北路路口(简称"北管制点")设立4处管制点。各类车辆到达管制点后,除持有博览会通行证的车辆、特种车辆、具有博览会专用车辆标志的出租车外,其余车辆均在管制点指定停靠点卸客,进入会展中心管制区的人员经安检后,乘坐免费摆渡车进入会展中心,摆渡车辆卸载乘客后根据交通疏导提示在管制点调头后在指定停靠点待客。

由于七道湾片区居民较多,展会期间交通管制措施将对该片区居民出行带来不便。为减少展会对该片区居民出行影响和分流部分米东南路路口管制点客流,允许1路、78路、532路公交车沿红光山路穿行,在"西管制点"与"东管制点"区域内严禁上下乘客。允许101路公交车(公交集团负责车内设安保人员)沿会展大道穿行,在"南管制点"与"东管制点"区域内严禁上下乘客,公交车辆持证通过。

常规1路公交车临时取消红光山、会展中心等站,并且临时增设七道湾路口(七道湾东街)、七道湾蔬菜公园等站;78路和532路临时取消红光山、会展中心等站;101路临时取消会展中心、会展纬六路、会展纬八路等站,上述线路待商博会结束后恢复正常。(参观群众和在会展中心管制区域内工作、居住的群众须在管制点下车后,乘坐摆渡车进入会展中心管制区域)。

1路、78路、532路公交车在米东大道西侧设立临时上客点,在南湖北路东侧设置临时下客点,在米东南路(由南向北方向)设立一处613路区间车临时停靠站;常规公交33路、105路、502路、527路和801路在七道湾路路口管制点附近,七道湾路"七道湾"公交站停靠上下客;518路、101路在龙盛街路口管制点附近,龙盛街"会展南区"公交站停靠上下客。

87

思考题：

1. 本案例中的国际会议交通管制措施具体有哪些？这样的国际会议交通管制措施与国外举行国际会议时有何区别？

2. 在本案例中，为了保障国际会议的顺利举行，进行了哪些公共交通管制和应对措施？这样的措施对中国其他城市举办国际会议有何启示？

Exercises
课后练习

1. 阅读材料，回答问题。

> In 2013, China's Foreign Minister Wang Yi's move marked the official return of the Hongqi and called Chinese officials to start using domestic cars instead of Western automobiles. The flagship Hongqi H7 were made available to private consumers as well starting May 30th. Chief manager of Beijing Hongqi Brand Wang Longfang noted a month after its launch:
>
> Over 20 cars have been sold in Beijing since they went on sale at the end of May. Provinces and central ministries have also passed orders. Sales could rise further as the production capacity increases. Our outlet in Beijing is located at the capital's luxury business circle, right next to many foreign luxury brands. Our outlet has attracted the biggest crowds...
>
> The Hongqi flagship model H7 sells between 300,000 yuan to 480,000 yuan. That's much lower than what you would pay for similar foreign luxury cars such as the Audi A6. And Hongqi's prospects for the future are good, as it is technologically advanced.

国际会议交通安排 | Traffic Arrangement of International Conference

  The new model L7 has also been put into use, and has transported foreign top officials such as the French President Francois Holland and South Korea's Park Geun-Hye, Business Insider remarks on the design and specifications of this new design:

  The L7 is a 6-meter (20-foot) dreadnought of an automobile, boasting a mammoth 12-cylinder engine and roughly resembling an oversized Bentley Flying Spur.

  Foreign dignitaries and officials above the rank of minister get the L7, while top-level Chinese officials are chauffeured in an even bigger version, the leviathan L9, which reportedly costs about $800,000 and looks like the kind of car rock stars might drive into swimming pools. Almost 40 centimeters (15 inches) longer than the L7, the L9 comes with an armored chassis, rear-opening "suicide doors" and an optional sun roof from which Chinese leaders emerge when reviewing troops.

  But the designs for the new Hongqiare completely domestic. The H7 is the first model solely developed, designed and manufactured by FAW, including testing, trial productions, and factory manufacturing. Even the engine is Chinese-made from scratch. With the revival of Hongqi, the state-owned auto manufacturing company FAW can hopefully raise the bar and public's enthusiasm for domestic automobiles. The Red Flag as a symbol of Communist Party privilege will probably limit its target consumers to Chinese bureaucrats, but FAW will invest 10.5 billion yuan through 2015 to make it China's official sedan.

  In 2014, during the APEC, Hongqi was chosen as the official sedan for the leaders around the world.

(1) What's will be the influence of Hongqi being selected as China's limousine to receive the foreign guests?

(2) What is the meaning for the reform of China's limousine, returned from western brand to Hongqi?

2. 根据下面的接机清单,分析其中可能存在的问题。

该接机单为重庆某大学举办国际学术研讨会,主办方前往江北国际机场接机时,工作人员的工作材料。

姓名	航班号	到达时间	联系电话	备注
24号到达(5人)				
TXY	CA1429	24日中午	139108432××	24号入住饭店
RYZ		24日到达		24号入住饭店
SKQ		24日到达		24号入住饭店
ZSX	MU5421	24日13:45	136615169××	自己预订宾馆
ZAG	ZH9168	24日11:50		无需住宿
25号上午到达(8人)				
DXL	CA1431	25日10:55	136813581××	考斯特车号218×× 王师傅 133896××
HL	CA1431	25日10:55	135529103××	
MYB	CA1431	25日10:55	136831264××	
LB	CA1431	25日10:30	136835903××	
ZSJ	CZ8102	25日11:50	135201778××	
ZZZ	CZ8102	25日11:50	135209000××	
JLY	CA1429	25日12:00	136712999××	
ZLL	CA 1429	25日12:00	139105730××	
25号下午到达(13人)				
WQB	CZ6549	25日12:45	135008007××	商务车63×× 马师傅 138083××
TC	CZ8214	25日13:40	135709319××	
PZQ	MU5421	25日13:45		
LP	MU2976	25日14:10	138882033××	
NZJ	CA4138	25日15:00	137011405××	
LKS	MU5425	25日15:20	159006578××	商务车74×× 申师傅13883××
TXH	CA1439	25日16:00	186118172××	
XHR		25日16:30	132603732××	

国际会议交通安排 | Traffic Arrangement of International Conference

HQN	SC4838	25日16:50	138064227××	商务车63×× 马师傅 1380834××
LBJ4人	CA1411	25日16:55	137013926××	
OB	SC4838	25日16:50	138064227××	
CYZ	MU2725	25日17:55	159962682××	小车93×× 杨师傅13983××
LYH	CA1435	25日18:55	136831869××	
25号晚上到达(12人)				
XLP	3U8974	25号20:35	13917075××	考斯特218×× 王师傅 13389679×××
ZGM	3U8974	25号20:35	13777882××	
SSY	FM9548	25日20:35		
WYX		25日21:10	13719058××	
SH	CA4144	25日21:15	13520003××	
GF	CA4144	25日21:15	13693580××	
WQB	CA4568	25日21:25	13500800××	
HFZ	CA4568	25日21.25	13944881××	
XZY	CA986	25日22:25	13611323××	小车26×× 刘师傅 1388355××
LXJ	CA986	25日22:25	13681222××	
ZFT		25日23:00	13699128××	自己打的去饭店
NY	PN6258	25日23:05	13834666××	要求派学生去接
重点嘉宾(2人)				
RZZ	来渝 25日 CA1439	13:30—16:00		学校单独迎接
	返京 27日 CA985	11:00—13:30		
WBY	来渝 25日 CA4138	12:30—15:00		小车67×× 舒师傅 1398393××
	返京 26日 CA4135	16:00—18:30		

91

为了实际研究需要,对真实姓名、联系方式、车牌号进行了匿名处理。

(1)根据所提供的材料,分析接机过程中可能存在的问题。

(2)如果存在这些问题,该如何改进。

(3)根据所学知识,结合本案例,请与会者设计一个操作性更强的接机表。

3. 阅读材料,回答问题

Beijing Grants Holidays to Workers for APEC Meeting

In an effort to ease traffic congestion and curb pollution, Beijing has already announced civil servants in the capital will be given six days off during the APEC meeting.

The Asia-Pacific Economic Cooperation (APEC) meeting will be held in Beijing from 5th to 11th November, 2014. In an effort to ease traffic congestions and curb pollution during this time, the Beijing Government is implementing the following initiatives:

• Civil servants in Beijing will be given six days off during APEC meeting

• Beijing city traffic will be limited from 2nd to 13th November

• Non Beijing license freighter truck will be not allowed to enter Beijing 6th ring area including into Huai Rou District during the whole event

• Beijing license freighter vehicles / trucks will be allowed to enter Beijing during the whole event from 24:00pm — 06:00am without any restriction as follow

• 0:00 to 03:00 hrs — uneven numbers

• 03:00 hrs to 06:00 hrs — even numbers

国际会议交通安排 | Traffic Arrangement of International Conference

（1）What is the impact of the holiday on the conference?

（2）Was the holiday created by China in this conference? If not, are there any countries take the similar measures?

4. 请列举至少5种与会者所知道的世界各国礼宾车，并用中英双语标出。

国别	车名	
	英文	中文

The Media Publicity of International Conference
国际会议媒体宣传

Overview
内容概览

For a large-scale international conference, the ultimate goal of media publicity is to enhance the brand of the conference, while promoting the host city's brand, or the brand of the sponsors for the conference. Media publicity is part of the international conference's Public Relations. This chapter will include exercises and further enhance the reader's ability to the media publicity of international conference.

对于大型国际会议而言，媒体宣传的最终目的是为了提升会议的品牌，同时拉动会议举办地的城市品牌，或会议赞助商的企业品牌。媒体宣传是国际会议筹划公关模块的一部分。本章主要从第一部分了解与媒体宣传相关的基础知识，通过对双语案例的解读来学习媒体宣传的安排，再通过实践操作和拓展阅读进一步提升读者的能力。

1. Basic Knowledge
基础知识

1.1 Introduction of Media 媒体宣传基础

In ancient times, the media refers to an intermediary matchmaker for marriages. Now it refers to information presentation and dissemination. The scope of the media is very broad, from books, pictures, models to film, television, radio, tape recorders, video recorders, videotapes, computer and various software.

国际会议媒体宣传 | The Media Publicity of International Conference

Four traditional media outlets are television, radio, newspapers and magazines. The new media outlets are IPTV, electronic magazines, micro-blogs, etc.

If one divides them according to the order in which they appear, newspapers and magazines are the first media, broadcast media is the second, television media is the third, the internet is the fourth, and mobile networks are known as the fifth media.

The Basic Definition of Media 媒体的基本定义

古时,媒指做媒,婚姻介绍的中介。现代人将其引用过来,指信息表示和传播的载体。媒体,即传播媒介、传播媒体,是指信息传播过程中,信息传播者与信息接收者之间的中介物,即存载并传递信息的载体和物质工具。从广义的角度讲,媒体的范畴是很广泛的,从书本、图片、模型到电影、电视、广播、录音机、录像机、录像带、计算机与各种软件等,都属于媒体的范畴。

The Category of Media 媒体的分类

媒体可分为传统媒体和新媒体。传统的四大媒体分别为电视、广播、报纸、杂志。新媒体有IPTV、电子杂志、微博、微信等。

如果按媒体出现的先后顺序来分,报纸刊物为第一媒体,广播为第二媒体,电视为第三媒体,互联网为第四媒体,移动网络为第五媒体。

1.2 Media Planning Process 媒体宣传计划流程

According to the purpose of the conference, the media plan varied from different levels. A full press publicity plan should include the theme, the make-up of the conference audience, media selection, the communication strategy, and the public information dissemination programs.

When promoting the event, do not request coverage and publicity from all media outlets, which is not only impossible but also unnecessary. Therefore, the media, consistent with the goals of the international conference, achieves the best publicity. Finally, the target is that media personnel should be assigned to different task. The list and phone number of relevant position in charge of media that best meet the requirements should be under record, and the reporter's list and phone number should be at hand.

After the media are filtered, staff responsible for media relations should begin contacting specific people and arranging interviews and press coverage according to the list. Those task includes the following perspective: contact media leaders and reporters, arrange the travel for correspondents, accommodations, make sure that there are no problems for media before or during the meeting..

After the media screening, people in charge of media should contact relevant media outlets to arrange interview times. First, the responsible person should contact the media leaders, and then restore to the designated reporter. When contacting reporters, it should be polite and have friendly relations for the media personnel. Finally, media personnel need to communicate with the on-scene reporters in order to ensure that media interviews during the meeting go on without any difficulty.

In early preparation, rally and warm-up are essential. Event organizers give full access to the network news and micro-bloggers because they have the ability to spread news widely and quickly at a low cost. Early in the meeting, when the preparatory work is basically completed, it is right moment to announce the main topic of the meeting.

After the warm-up, event organizers should be ready for the news material, arrange interviews from different perspectives for different media, so as to make journalism and publicity go smoothly during the meeting.

Develop Media Plans 制订媒体宣传计划

根据国际会议的嘉宾、会议所要达到的效果、覆盖范围来拟定不同层次的计划。完整的新闻宣传计划应包括分析会议主题、会议受众，选择媒体，设定传播路线，确定传播策略，拟定新闻宣传传播方案。

Filter Media 筛选媒体

在筛选媒体时，首先列出主要媒体名单。根据新闻宣传目标，列出中央级媒体、举办会议的地方级媒体，有必要列出会议所涉及范围内的国外媒体，并进行分类处理。

会议的宣传，不能强求所有媒体报道与宣传，这既不现实也会造成不必要的浪费。所以要根据现有资源，筛选出最符合本次国际会议目标的媒体，力求以最精简的媒体达到最好的宣传效果。最后，要具体到媒体人员。记录下最符合要求的媒体的相关负责人、记者的名单与联系电话。

国际会议媒体宣传 | The Media Publicity of International Conference

Contact Media 联系媒体

媒体筛选出来以后，负责媒体联系的人员就开始根据名单进行具体的联系、对接工作。包括联系媒体负责人和记者，安排好记者的行程、食宿问题，确保会议举办期间媒体采访万无一失。

Communication and Coordination 沟通协调

媒体筛选结束后，负责媒体联系的人员就应该与相关媒体进行沟通、对接相应的工作。首先联系媒体负责人，接着联系媒体负责人指定的记者。在与记者联系时，要礼貌得体，与媒体人员保持友好关系。最后要与赴现场的记者进行沟通，确保会议期间媒体采访万无一失。

Early Preheat 前期预热

在前期的准备过程中，一定的造势和预热是必不可少的。可以充分发挥网络新闻、微博传播范围广，速度快，成本低的特点。在会议召开前期，各项准备工作基本就绪，宣布会议的主要议题等内容，可为会议的召开做好良好的铺垫。

Prepare Manuscript 准备稿件

前期预热之后，最好提前准备好新闻素材，拟定新闻标题，针对不同媒体安排不同的采访角度，有利于会议的新闻宣传正常有序进行。

1.3 Media Area 媒体采访区

The media interview area should not be held too far away from the venue, because during the conference, media personnel often invite guests out of the venue to be interviewed.

According to the different aspects of media, we can choose different interview environments. Television media interviews are preferably arranged in locations with good lighting, less noise, and a relatively independent space. Newspapers, magazines and the like can be selected in relatively casual places, such as lounges, cafes, etc.

When entering into various interview locations, the reporters and the carried equipment should be subject to security checks. It is forbidden to carry weapons, as well as inflammable and explosive materials. According to relevant regulations, media personnel should take measures to prohibit any unauthorized materials from being allowed into the interview space. During press conferences, the television reporter and photographer's tripods should be placed in the specified location and the recorder of the text reporter can be placed next to the speakers.

Location Requirements 位置要求

媒体采访区不宜离会场太远,因为在会议过程中,媒体工作人员往往会邀请嘉宾走出会场接受采访。

Environmental Requirements 环境要求

根据不同媒体的不同特点,可以选择不同的采访环境。电视媒体的采访最好安排采光好、噪音少、空间相对独立的空间。报纸、杂志之类的采访可以选择相对休闲的场所,比如休息室、咖啡厅等。

Equipment Requirements 设备要求

进入各种采访活动现场的记者及所携带的设备均需经过安检。严禁携带武器和易燃、易爆物品以及与采访活动无关的物品。新闻发布会、记者会时,电视记者和摄影记者的三角架应安放在指定位置,文字记者的袖珍录音机可放在音箱旁。

2. Case Study
案例分析

2.1 Case Summary 案例概述

本章选择中外两则案例展示国际会议的媒体宣传。第一则英文案例展示的是国外在承办国际会议时进行媒体宣传的策略。第二则中文案例展示了中国在承办国际会议时进行的媒体宣传策略和实施方式。

2.2 2014 International AIDS Conference

Case Guide-Reading 案例导读

This case is based on the traffic arrangement of AIDS Conference. With the demonstration of the media plan for this conference, it provides the basic contents about the media publicity of the international conference for the reader.

国际会议媒体宣传 | The Media Publicity of International Conference

The XX International AIDS Conference was held in Melbourne, Australia from 20 to 25 July 2014 at the Melbourne Convention and Exhibition Centre. It was organized by the International AIDS Society (IAS). Over 14,000 scientists, campaigners and politicians were expected to attend.

......

Media Centre
AIDS 2014 Programme
Programme-at-a-Glance

The entire AIDS 2014 programme is available online through the online Programme-at-a-Glance (PAG) — so you can see who is presenting what, when.

You can view all conference sessions and speakers, abstract titles and presenters, programme activities and satellites. Links to abstracts, slide presentations, videos, rapporteur reports and e-posters will be added as they become available.

Online app

A faster and more streamlined mobile app is also available this year; the app is available for download on the Apple App Store and Google Play store. By logging onto the App, you will be able to retrieve your itinerary made on the online version of the Programme-at-a-Glance.

Photos and Videos
Online Photo Library

Free, high resolution photos for use by the media and others (with appropriate credit) are available on our online gallery.

YouTube Channel

Videos featuring conference highlights, interviews with key speakers and delegates as well as recorded sessions are available on the conference YouTube Channel.

Resources for Journalists

Media Guide

The AIDS 2014 Media Guide describes the onsite facilities that will be available to accredited journalists in Melbourne and includes practical information to help plan your coverage of the conference.

Background Information

Fact sheets and other background information, including programme highlights, are available here.

Partner Coverage
FHI 360

FHI 360 provided live coverage of digital content being shared on social media such as tweets, posts, digital and hashtag campaigns, op-eds, blogs and more during the conference.

AIDS 2014 Live Recap Archives

AIDS 2014 Live Social Blog

AIDS 2014 Live Hub

AIDS 2014 Live Video Interviews

AIDS 2014 TV

In partnership with the broadcasting company WebsEdge, the conference provided an on-site AIDS 2014 TV channel featuring programme highlights and interviews.

News Reports by NAM

NAM offered news stories on major scientific presentations and hosted online discussion forums for HIV implementers. NAM also published a free daily news bulletin in English and translated into French, Portuguese, Spanish and Russian.

Scientific Analysis by CCO

Clinical Care Options' (CCO) is the official online provider of scientific analysis for delegates and journalists including expert audio highlights, capsule summaries of important clinical data, downloadable slidesets, and more.

国际会议媒体宣传 | The Media Publicity of International Conference

> **Conference Blog**
>
> Lights, camera, but where's the ACTION? Crimina...Jul 25 2014
>
> Now or Never: The Urgency of Closing the Treatm...Jul 25 2014
>
> **The Daily Bulletin**
>
> News and information from each day of the conference is available through the Daily Bulletin.

Analysis and Summary 分析概要

This case is selected from 2014 International AIDS Conference which fully indicates the overall performance of the media for this conference. In this case, the media center, media plan, online tool and social media are well prepared by the organizer. The media schedule can be recognized as the case of the media publicity in international conference.

Questions 思考题

1. What are the measures for the media plan in this conference?
2. Compared with conference at home, what are the specialties for the media publicity in this conference?

2.3 关于举办2014中国边贸战略与发展高峰论坛暨26国国际投资峰会的通知

Case Guide-Reading 案例导读

本文属于一则有关国际会议媒体宣传的中文案例。该案例较为详细地阐述了国际会议媒体报道的诸多方面。通过对本案例的学习,读者可以较为直观和全面地掌握国内举办的国际会议媒体宣传的基本内容和特色。

> 为贯彻党中央国务院"全方位、多层次、宽领域"的对外开放政策和"走出去请进来"的战略,搞好同周边国家的关系……由中华人民共和国商务部为指导单位,中国国际贸易促进委员会特别支持单位……等单位共同举办的2014中国边贸(深圳)战略与发展高峰论坛暨26国国际投资峰会。

2014年中国外贸发展的国内外环境略好于2013年,但面临的困难和风险依然较多,国际市场需求总体偏弱,各国产业间竞争日益激烈,贸易摩擦形势依然严峻……

峰会特色
　　1. 高层次、高端化……
　　2. 专区化、专业化……
　　3. 更直接、更高效……

峰会优势
　　1. 品牌优势……
　　2. 资源优势……
　　3. 运作优势……
　　4. 活动优势……
　　5. 宣传优势……
　　6. 服务优势……

组织机构
　　主办单位:
　　中华人民共和国商务部
　　广东省人民政府
　　深圳市人民政府
　　中国国际贸易促进委员会
　　……
　　承办单位:
　　深圳乾宏文化管理有限公司
　　中国香港美术家协会
　　《中国边贸》杂志社
　　长沙市红中文化传媒有限公司
　　协办单位:
　　广东省商务厅
　　深圳市委宣传部
　　……

国际会议媒体宣传 | The Media Publicity of International Conference

> 支持单位：
> 辽宁省商务厅
> 吉林省商务厅
> 黑龙江商务厅
> ……
> 特别支持单位：
> 中国国际投资者联合会、世界华人华商联合会……
> 论坛主题：
> 服务边贸创新发展共享共赢
> 邀请宣传媒体：
> 1. 报纸媒体
> 综合类：人民日报、环球时报、文汇报、大公报、南华早报、星岛日报、联合早报……
> 专业类：中国旅游报、中国文化报、中国民族报……
> 2. 新闻杂志
> 中国边贸杂志、商业周刊、财经、第一财经周刊……
> 3. 网络媒体
> 中国边贸网、网易、新浪网、央视网、东方财富网、和讯网……
> 4. 广播电视媒体
> 中央人民广播电台、中国国际广播电台、第一财经频道、中央电视台……
> 5. 通讯社
> 国内：新华社广东分社、中新社。
> 国外：美联社、路透社、彭博新闻社、法新社、韩联社。
> 6. 地方新闻媒体
> 深圳广播电台、深圳电视台。
> 以中央级及省级媒体组成的新闻媒体联盟和媒体支持单位为核心，组成"论坛"媒体战略合作联盟，配合宣传"论坛"各项主题活动。

Analysis and Summary 分析概要

该案例选取一个中文国际会议作为样本，较为全面地展现了国内举办国际会议的媒体宣传工作。由该案例可以看出,国内有关单位进行国际会议媒体宣传时较为注重承办单位、参与嘉宾级、合作单位和媒体性质等方面的内容。该案例是国内有关单位举办国际会议时媒体宣传的通行做法,很有代表性。

Questions 思考题

1. 在该案例中,参与本次国际会议的媒体有哪几类?
2. 在该案例中,国际会议的媒体报道与一般国外举办的国际会议媒体报道有何差异?

2.4 Case Comparison 案例对比

会议名称	2014中国边贸战略与发展高峰论坛暨26国国际投资峰会	2014 International AIDS Conference
媒体支持	报纸媒体 新闻杂志 网络媒体等	ABC News etc.
新媒体	微博等	Online app, The Daily Bulletin, AIDS 2014 TV
报道效果	低	低

Analysis and Summary 分析概要

　　根据国际会议媒体宣传的基本内容,案例对比将所选择的中文和英文案例分块进行比较,以突显中外进行国际会议媒体宣传时各项具体工作中的异同。

Questions 思考题

1. 通过上述两个案例的学习,可否明确国际会议媒体宣传的主要内容?
2. 上述两份国际会议媒体报道在主要内容上有何异同?
3. 上述两份国际会议媒体报道主要内容有何内在联系?

国际会议媒体宣传 | The Media Publicity of International Conference

3. Supplementary Reading
拓展阅读

3.1 1936 Berlin Olympics

The 1936 Summer Olympics, officially known as the Games of the XI Olympiad, was an international multi-sport event that was held in 1936 in Berlin, Germany. Berlin won the bid to host the Games over Barcelona, Spain, on 26 April 1931, at the 29th IOC Session in Barcelona (two years before the Nazis came to power). It marked the second and final time that the International Olympic Committee would gather to vote in a city which was bidding to host those Games. The only other time this occurred was at the inaugural IOC Session in Paris, France, on 24 April 1894. Then, Athens and Paris were chosen to host the 1896 and 1900 Games, respectively.

To outdo the Los Angeles games of 1932, Germany built a new 100,000-seat track and field stadium, six gymnasiums, and many other smaller arenas. They also installed a closed-circuit television system and radio network that reached 41 countries, with many other forms of expensive high-tech electronic equipment. Filmmaker Leni Riefenstahl, a favourite of Adolf Hitler, was commissioned by the German Olympic Committee to film the Games for $7 million. Her film, titled Olympia, pioneered many of the techniques now common in the filming of sports.

Hitler saw the Games as an opportunity to promote his government and ideals of racial supremacy, and the official Nazi party paper, the Völkischer Beobachter, wrote in the strongest terms that Jews and Black people should not be allowed to participate in the Games. However, when threatened with a boycott of the Games by other nations, he relented and allowed Black people and Jews to participate, and added one token participant to the German team—a German woman, Helene Mayer, who had a Jewish father. At the same time, the party removed signs stating "Jews not wanted" and similar slogans from the city's main tourist attractions. In an attempt to "clean up" Berlin, the German Ministry of the Interior authorized the chief of police to arrest all Romani (Gypsies) and keep them in a "special camp," the Berlin-Marzahn concentration camp. Total ticket revenues were 7.5 million Reichsmark, generating a profit of over one million marks. The official budget did not include outlays by the city of Berlin (which issued an itemized report detailing its costs of 16.5 million marks) or outlays of the German national government (which did not make its costs public, but is estimated to have spent US$30 million, chiefly in capital outlays).

Hans von Tschammer und Osten, as Reichssportführer, i.e. head of the Deutscher Reichsbundfür Leibesübungen (DRL), the Reich Sports Office, played a major role in the structure and organization of the Olympics. He promoted the idea that the use of sports would harden the German spirit and instill unity among German youth. At the same time he also believed that sports was a "way to weed out the weak, Jewish, and other undesirables."

Von Tschammer trusted the details of the organization of the games to Theodor Lewald and Carl Diem, the former president and secretary of the Deutscher Reichsausschussfür Leibesübungen, the forerunner of the Reich Sports Office. Among Diem's ideas for the Berlin Games was the introduction of the Olympic torch relay between Greece and the host nation.

The German Olympic committee, in accordance with Nazi directives, virtually barred Germans who were Jewish or Roma or had such an ancestry from participating in the Games (Helene Mayer was the only German Jew to compete at the Berlin Games). This decision meant exclusion for many of the country's top athletes such as shotputter and discus thrower Lilli Henoch, who was a four-time world record holder and 10-time German national champion, and Gretel Bergmann who was suspended from the German team just days after she set a record of 1.60 meters in the high jump.

During the Games, Hauptmann Wolfgang Fürstner, the commandant of the Olympic Village in Wustermark, was abruptly replaced by

国际会议媒体宣传 | The Media Publicity of International Conference

> Oberstleutnant Werner von Gilsa, commander of the Berlin Guard-Regiment. The official reason given by the Nazis was that Fürstner had not acted "with the necessary energy" after 370,000 visitors had passed through the village — between 1 May to 15 June — causing significant damage to the site. However this reason was just a pretext to disparaging the half-Jewish officer and expediting his removal[citation needed]. Fürstner committed suicide shortly after the conclusion of the Berlin Olympics because he learned the Nuremberg Laws classified him as a Jew. As such, the career officer was to be expelled from the Wehrmacht.

Blank-filling

Directions: Complete each brackets with appropriate words or phrases from the passage.

  Germany built a new and huge (　　). They installed radio network and (　　) that reached some countries, with many other forms of expensive high-tech electronic equipment. Filmmaker was commissioned by the German Olympic Committee to film the Games for $7 million. Her film pioneered many of the techniques in the current filming of (　　).

Questions and Answers

Directions: In this part there is one question. You need to ask the question based on the words or phrases from the passage.

What is the specialty of the advertisement in this Olympic game in Germany? And did these activities cause any problems?

3.2 北京2008年奥运会场馆媒体中心

>   北京2008年奥运会场馆媒体中心是2008年奥运会专为媒体而设立的中心，它是北京奥运会媒体报道工作的大本营——主新闻中心（MPC）和国际广播中心（IBC）的所在地。场馆媒体中心运行的目标是为注册的文字和摄影记者提供最好的工作环境，以便他们成功报道奥运会。其工作的依据是国际奥委会技术手册的要求和往届奥运会的标准。

国际广播中心(IBC)外观和主新闻中心(MPC)外观

通过与国际奥委会的多次商讨,北京奥运会各场馆媒体中心的容量已经确定,并于2006年8月12日得到了国际奥委会的确认。场馆媒体中心的容量的确定遵循了往届奥运会的经验,并综合考虑了各场馆的具体情况和体育项目在中国的发展情况。场馆媒体中心团队负责北京31个场馆媒体中心运行的运行,并负责协调6个京外协办城市,即青岛(帆船)和香港(马术)以及上海、天津、秦皇岛和沈阳等四个足球比赛城市的媒体运行工作。

主新闻中心中央发布厅和文字记者工作间

此外,场馆媒体中心团队还负责三个非竞赛场馆媒体中心的计划和运行工作。现在,场馆媒体中心运行的筹备工作正在由计划阶段向场馆化阶段进行转换。场馆媒体中心的工作人员与场馆设计者和业主,以及北京奥组委场馆团队紧密合作,以保证媒体在各场馆中的不同需求得到满足,同时确保媒体设施和服务达到国际奥委会的要求及往届奥运会的惯例。

国际会议媒体宣传 | The Media Publicity of International Conference

问答

2008北京奥运会新闻报道的基地在何处?

制图

请绘制一幅新闻中心与相关城市和赛场媒体中心的逻辑图,以展现北京奥运会新闻媒体报道中心的体系。

Exercises
课后练习

1. 请列举至少6个古今中外国际会议媒体宣传的经典案例。

国别	媒体宣传案例

2. 奥斯卡金像奖

Academy Awards

Each January, the entertainment community and film fans around the world turn their attention to the Academy Awards. Interest and anticipation builds to a fevered pitch leading up to the Oscar telecast in February, when hundreds of millions of movie lovers tune in to watch the glamorous ceremony and learn who will receive the highest honors in filmmaking.

It is an annual American awards ceremony honoring cinematic

109

achievements in the film industry. The various category winners are awarded a copy of a statuette, officially the Academy Award of Merit, which is better known by its nickname Oscar. The awards, first presented in 1929 at the Hollywood Roosevelt Hotel, are overseen by the Academy of Motion Picture Arts and Sciences (AMPAS).

  The awards ceremony was first televised in 1953 and is now seen live in more than 200 countries. The Oscars is the oldest entertainment awards ceremony; its equivalents, the Emmy Awards for television, the Tony Awards for theatre, and the Grammy Awards for music and recording, are modeled after the Academy Awards. The Academy Awards are widely considered to be the most prestigious cinema awards ceremony in the world.

(1) What is the media's positive influence on the Oscar?

(2) Could you list the name of Chinese actor(s) or actress(es) who acquire the reputation through Academy Awards?

3. Reading the information on the IOC Social Media, Blogging and Internet Guidelines for participants and other accredited persons at the Sochi 2014 Olympic Winter Games.

Frequently Asked Questions

Q: Who is concerned by the Guidelines?

A: The Guidelines apply to all accredited persons, in particular to all athletes, coaches, officials, personnel of National Olympic Committees and International Federations and members of media accredited to the Olympic Games ("Participants").

Q: When do the Guidelines apply?

A: The Guidelines apply from the opening of the Olympic Villages (30

国际会议媒体宣传 | The Media Publicity of International Conference

January 2014), until the closing of the Olympic Villages (26 February 2014).

Q: Can I use social media or update my blog/website during my participation in the Olympic Games?

A: YES; the IOC encourages Participants to blog about their experience at the Olympic Games but requests that certain rules are observed. In particular, Participants' activities on social media and the internet should comply with the Olympic Charter and be consistent with the Olympic values of "Friendship, Excellence and Respect." Also remember that any online activity is still subject to applicable laws (such as defamation, privacy and intellectual property laws) and so the Guidelines require Participants to respect those laws and ensure that their social media activity is in good taste, dignified and does not contain vulgar or obscene content. Postings that are racist, discriminatory or otherwise offensive towards other Participants or third parties are also forbidden under the Guidelines. During the period of the Olympic Games, Participants are not allowed to commercialize their social media and internet activity (see further below "Can I post about my sponsors during the Olympic Games?").

Q: Can I post about the competitions?

A: YES; Participants can post about their participation in the competitions, other competitions or their experiences generally during the Olympic Games, but they should not assume the role of a journalists or media outlet. Posting should hence be in first-person, diary-type format. In their online activities, Participants must not disclose any information which is confidential or private in relation to any other person or organization involved in the Olympic Games.

Q: Can I answer questions from the media asked through internet or social media?

A: YES; in the same way as offline, Participants are allowed — but under no obligation — to answer questions from the media asked through internet or social media. Participants should also be vigilant about their postings and keep in mind that what they say and post on the internet and social media will be in the public domain and may be used by the media.

Q: Can I share photos taken from Olympic venues?

A: YES; Participants can share still photographs taken within or outside competition venues and other Olympic venues on social media and internet provided such postings are not used for commercial purposes and respect applicable laws and the rights of others. Please note that specific requirements apply in the perimeter of the Olympic Villages (see below "Can I post photos or videos taken within the Olympic Villages?").

Q: Can I share videos taken from Olympic Venues?

A: Participants can record video or audio content within or outside competition venues and other Olympic venues, with non-professional recording material (no TV equipment, tripods or monopods are allowed). However, video or audio content taken from within Olympic venues (including from within the Olympic Villages or the Olympic Park) must only be for personal use and must not be uploaded or shared on any website, blog, social media page, public photo- or video-sharing sites or mobile application. Participants can share video or audio content taken outside competition venues and other Olympic venues on social media and the internet provided that such posting is not for commercial purposes and respect applicable laws and the rights of others.

Q: Can I post photos or videos taken within the Olympic Villages?

A: YES; Participants can take photos within the Olympic Villages (except in areas designated as "no picture areas") and such photos can be posted on the internet or social media. However, it is important to

国际会议媒体宣传 | The Media Publicity of International Conference

keep in mind that if another person's image is included or referred to in a posting, such person's permission should be obtained beforehand. Videos or audio content recorded within the Olympic Village must only be for personal use and must not be uploaded or shared on any website, blog, social media page, public photo- or video-sharing sites or mobile application. Persons staying in the Olympic Villages are also required to respect the protected atmosphere of the Olympic Villages and are not allowed to report on the activities of other residents, unless they have obtained such other persons' consent beforehand.

Q: Can I post about my sponsors during the Olympic Games?

A: NO; Unless they have obtained the prior written approval of the IOC or their NOC, Participants must not, either promote any brand, product or service on their social media pages, blogs or personal websites, or use social media and internet in a manner that creates or implies any association between the Olympic Games or the IOC and a third party, or its products and services. All competitors, coaches, trainers and officials must ensure that their activities on the internet and social media comply with the requirements of Rule 40 of the Olympic Charter and the related instructions issued by the IOC, Sochi 2014 and their respective National Olympic Committees.

Q: Can I use the Olympic symbol or other Olympic properties in my internet and social media posts?

A: Participants and other accredited persons are not allowed to use the Olympic symbol (the five interlocking rings) in their postings, blogs or tweets. Only members of accredited media are authorized to use the Olympic symbol for factual and news editorial purposes, for example in a news article covering the Olympic Games. The word "Olympic" and other Olympic-related terminology can be used by Participants in their social media and internet activities but only for editorial/factual purposes (for example to describe and report about their experience at

> the Games). The use of the Sochi 2014 emblem or mascots is subject to the prior written approval of Sochi 2014, while the use of the NOC emblems is subject to the relevant NOCs. In any event, the Olympic symbol and other Olympic properties must not be used for commercial purposes, or in a manner that suggests any kind of endorsement by the IOC or Sochi 2014. The Olympic symbol and other Olympic properties should be used in their normal design or wording.

(1) Compared with other organizations, what is the meaning of media report for Olympic Games?

(2) What are the methods for the new media in this report?

The Marketing of International Conference
国际会议市场开发

Overview
内容概览

Marketing is the activity, with set of institutions and processes which is valuable for relevant stakeholders. Marketing links the public through opportunities and problems. The marketing of international conference is an activity based on the market development of the conference.

国际会议的市场开发关系到会议的经费来源、会议规模、影响能力等,能扩大国际会议对国家、城市、各企业的影响力,是国际会议取得成功的重要因素之一。国际会议市场开发包括会议赞助的策划、实施,以及国际会议的营销策略。

在选择传递会议消息的办法时,要充分考虑各自的优劣,结合实际情况,如会议规模、经费、实效性等进行筛选。会议营销特点的多样性决定了其内容的丰富性。

1. Basic Knowledge
基础知识

1.1 The Market Development of Conference 会议的市场开发

The marketing of conference refers to specific objectives, with a corresponding strategy to attract the attention.

The marketing of international conference includes meetings sponsored by the planning and implementation of marketing strategy, which expands the international conference's influence on countries, cities, each enterprise, etc.

The Meaning of the Market Development on Conference 会议市场开发的涵义

会议市场开发是指针对特定的对象,制定相应的推广会议的策略方案,从而达到会议想要达到的效果及其附带收益。

The Content of the Market Development on Conference 国际会议市场开发的内容

国际会议市场开发包括会议赞助的策划及实施和国际会议的营销策略,扩大国际会议对国家、城市、各企业的影响力。

Print advertising refers to the way in which meeting planners advertise the meeting in the form of text printing. Printed advertisements must be concise and clear. There should be a conference logo, pictures, phone, fax, email and address. Printed advertisement is a very good method of advertising, and must be attractive. It has a long tradition, but the price is high.

The second marketing method is direct mail. One should consider printing and postage costs. Effective direct mailing requires a mailing list which must be up-to-date and on which the addresses must be accurate and correct. Mailing lists can be gotten from any industry associations or other places. For direct mail, organizer can try to send a postcard first, and then send a detailed leaflet, booklet, report, or registration information.

The third method is telephone marketing. This method is usually used about two months before attending the meeting. The personnel make phone calls to the potential participants, remind them of the time of the meeting, and allow them to register by phone. Telemarketing has a big advantage. It provides the opportunity for a human connection between the participants and opportunities. Print advertising and direct mail are passive methods. Print advertising is possible only when the participants see it.

Internet marketing is a more popular method in recent years, and is likely to be extremely attractive and one of the widely used methods. Electronic marketing can save a lot of money. Using electronic marketing, one can send emails directly and provide the relevant information in the email link. Although the electronic marketing can't replace the human connection of telephone marketing, at least email can play a role in reminding potential participants of

国际会议市场开发 | The Marketing of International Conference

the upcoming event. Registration can be in the form of PDF file as an email attachment or directly as an e-mail sent to potential participants. The attendee can, therefore, respond and register directly.

The only drawback of e-mail is the spam folder. When you use electronic marketing and send the same emails to a group, you must make sure the information sent will not be treated as spam.

Print Advertising 印刷品广告

印刷品广告是指会议策划者利用文字印刷的形式来宣传会议。印刷品广告必须简明扼要、条理清楚，应该有会议的会标、图片、电话、传真、电子邮件和网址等联系方式。印刷品广告必须能够吸引和保持人们的注意力。印刷品广告是一种很好的广告方法，它具有持续时间长的特点，但是价格也不菲。

Mail Directly 直接邮寄

第二种方法是直接邮寄。直接邮寄不受篇幅的影响。当然，信息同样要做到简明扼要。虽然从某种程度上说，直接邮寄可以传送任何信息，但是仍然要考虑印刷和邮资费用。直接邮寄需要准备一个邮寄名单，邮寄名单必须是最新的，而且地址必须准确无误。邮寄名单可以从产业协会或其他地方买到。直接邮寄，可以先寄一张明信片试试，然后再寄上一份内容详细的广告单或小册子，并附上报到注册信息。

Telephone Marketing 电话营销

传递信息的第三种方法是电话营销。这种方法一般在会议召开前两个月左右使用。电话营销人员打电话给潜在的与会者，提醒他们会议的时间，并试图让他们通过电话来注册。电话营销一个很大的优点是提供了和与会者之间的真人联系机会。印刷品广告和直接邮寄都是被动的方法。印刷品广告登出后只有在与会者看到时才有可能起作用；直接邮寄也要在潜在与会者打开阅读时才能起作用。

Electronic Marketing 电子营销

电子营销是近年来比较流行的一种方法，且很可能成为极有吸引力并被广泛采用的方法之一。电子营销可以节约很多开支。电子营销可以直接发电子邮件，也可以在电子邮件中提供相关信息的链接。尽管电子营销不能取代电话营销的真人联系，但至少可以起到提醒作用。可以将注册表以PDF

117

文件形式随电子邮件附件或直接作为电子邮件发送给潜在与会者,与会者可以直接进行回复和注册。

电子邮件唯一的缺点是垃圾邮件问题。当与会者使用电子营销方式给一个群组发送相同邮件时,必须要确定所发送信息不被当作垃圾邮件处理。

1.2 Conference Marketing 会议营销

Organizer needs to analyze, grasp and use the inherent law of meeting marketing. It was concluded by the practitioner as the following seven conference marketing characteristics: (1) culture; (2) concept; (3) strategy; (4) pertinence; (5) effectiveness; (6) permeability; (7) transmission.

The main contents of conference marketing are as follows: (1) selecting the meeting selection; (2) the theme and purpose of the meeting establishment; (3) propaganda before meeting; (4) slogan; (5) preparation before the meeting; (6) pick-up; (7) meeting services; (8) corporate image; (9) press release writing and publishing. (10) gift-giving; (11) customer information collection and processing.

The Characteristic of Conference Marketing 会议营销的特点

会议营销内在的规律,需要我们去分析、掌握和运用。精细管理工程创始人刘先明归纳的会议营销的特点,有以下七个:(1)文化性强;(2)概念性强;(3)战略性强;(4)针对性强;(5)有效性强;(6)渗透性强;(7)传播性强。

The Content of Conference Marketing 会议营销的主要工作内容

会议营销的主要内容如下:(1)优选会议;(2)确立会议和会议营销的主题和目的;(3)会前宣传工作;(4)撰写和展示广告语;(5)会前的各项会务准备工作;(6)接站工作;(7)会场服务;(8)企业形象展示;(9)撰写新闻稿件,及时发表;(10)会议礼品的确立和赠送;(11)客户信息的搜集、整理。

2. Case Study 案例分析

2.1 Case Summary 案例概述

本章选取中外两则案例来展现国际会议的市场开发问题。第一则英文

国际会议市场开发 | The Marketing of International Conference

案例是意大利米兰世博会的市场开发计划,体现了国际会议市场开发的最新动态。第二则中文案例是北京奥运会的市场开发计划,全面展现了中国举办国际会议的市场开发新举措。

2.2 2015 Italy World Expo

Case Guide-Reading 案例导读

This case is based on the conference marketing of Italy World Expo. With the fully demonstration of the market development for this conference, it provides the diversified contents about the marketing of the international conference for the reader.

> Expo 2015 is the next scheduled Universal Exposition after Expo 2012, and will be hosted by Milan, Italy.
>
> **Theme**
>
> The theme chosen for the 2015 Milan Universal Exposition is Feeding the Planet, Energy for Life. This embraces technology, innovation, culture, traditions and creativity and how they relate to food and diet. Expo 2015 will further develop themes introduced in earlier Expos (e.g., water at Expo 2008 in Zaragoza) in the light of new global scenarios and emerging issues, with a principal focus on the right to healthy, secure and sufficient food for all the world's inhabitants.
>
> There are seven proposed sub-themes:
>
> Science for Food Safety, Security and Quality
>
> Innovation in the Agro Food Supply Chain
>
> Technology for Agriculture and Biodiversity
>
> Dietary Education
>
> Solidarity and Cooperation on Food
>
> Food for Better Lifestyles
>
> Food in the World's Cultures and Ethnic Groups
>
> **Mascot**
>
> The Expo Milano 2015 mascot, Foody, embodies the key themes of

Image from the homepage of the Expo Milano 2015

the event in a way that's upbeat, original and powerful. The mascot characters are: Guaglió, the Garlic — Arabella, the Orange — Josephine, the Banana — Gury, the Watermelon — Pomina, the Apple — Max Maize, the Blue Corn — Manghy, the Mango — Rodolfo, the Fig — Piera, the Pear — Rap Brothers, the Radishes — Chicca, the Pomegranate.

Partners

Expo Milano 2015 offers a unique business opportunity. The support of the business community is paramount, not only during the preparation phase but also during the six months that the exhibition takes place.

Leading businesses in innovation, technology, energy, mobility, security and banking have decided to become partners of the event and it is thanks to these companies and their valuable contribution that Expo Milano 2015 will be able to offer an unforgettable experience to everyone who visits.

Partners are categorized by three different levels of involvement within the exhibition: Official Global Partner, Premium Partner and Official Partner.

Profiles of the Official Partners of Expo 2015 S.p.A. and the services provided by them for this event are available within the Official Partners Catalogue.

Official Global Partners

Official Global Partners are companies whose activities and values are intrinsically linked to the theme of the Expo Milan 2015, and which

国际会议市场开发 | The Marketing of International Conference

make a considerable contribution to the development of the theme. Global leaders in their fields, these companies provide the main services and technology for the event, supporting the core values of innovation and sustainability.

Investment range: Cash + VIK >20 million euro.

Official Global Airline Carriers

Leading players in the air transport sector at national and international level will ensure competitive and efficient services for Visitors, and help facilitate travel from all over the world and across Italy.

Official Premium Partners

Official Premium Partners are companies and organizations that are involved in key projects such as themed pavilions. Alternatively they may offer their know-how, products and services for the construction and running of the Exhibition Site or contribute to the overall success of the event.

Investment range: Cash + VIK: 10 to 20 million euro.

Official Global Rail Carriers

Supporting rail Visitors to Expo Milano 2015, a number of important partnerships have been opened with leading operators in the field, which will make available their strengths and skills for the Event.

Official Partners

Some of these companies and organizations will collaborate on key projects such as the Clusters or other important elements of Expo Milan 2015, while others provide products and services for the construction and running of the Exhibition Site or contribute to the overall success of the event.

Investment range: Cash + VIK 3 to 10 million Euro.

Sponsor

Expo Milano 2015 offers companies new communication opportunities, increasing their recognition and visibility on the international stage. As Official Sponsors, companies promote one of the Expo themes, supporting Universal Exposition projects.

Image from the homepage of the Expo Milano 2015

Analysis and Summary 分析概要

This case is selected from 2015 Italy World Expo which indicates the overall performance of the marketing for this conference. In this case, the multi-type partners and sponsors are carefully selected by the organizer. The market development can be recognized as the representative of the conference marketing.

Questions 思考题

What are the types for partners and sponsors for this World Expo?

Compared with conference at home, what are the specialties for the conference marketing?

国际会议市场开发 | The Marketing of International Conference

2.3 2008北京奥运会市场开发计划

Case Guide-Reading 案例导读

本文属于一则有关国际会议市场开发的中文案例。在该案例中较为详细地阐述了国际会议市场开发的诸多方面。通过对本案例的学习,读者可以较为直观和全面地掌握国内举办的国际会议市场开发的基本内容、模式和特色。

第一部分 北京2008年奥运会赞助计划

……

一、宗旨

……

二、赞助层次

……

北京2008年奥运会赞助计划包括三个层次:

北京2008年奥运会合作伙伴

北京2008年奥运会赞助商

北京2008年奥运会供应商(独家供应商/供应商)

……

三、赞助商权益

赞助企业向北京奥组委、中国奥委会和中国奥运代表团直接提供有力的资金和实物支持。作为回报,赞助企业将享有相应的权益。以下是北京奥组委给予赞助企业的主要回报方式:

—— 使用北京奥组委和/或中国奥委会的徽记和称谓进行广告和市场营销活动;

—— 享有特定产品/服务类别的排他权利;

—— 获得奥运会的接待权益,包括奥运会期间的住宿、证件、开闭幕式及比赛门票,使用赞助商接待中心等;

—— 享有奥运会期间电视广告及户外广告的优先购买权;

—— 享有赞助文化活动及火炬接力等主题活动的优先选择权;

—— 参加北京奥组委组织的赞助商研讨考察活动;

——北京奥组委实施赞助商识别计划和鸣谢活动；
——北京奥组委实施防范隐性市场计划,保护赞助商权益；

根据对奥林匹克运动和北京奥运会贡献的价值不同,合作伙伴、赞助商和供应商享有不同的权益回报。

四、赞助销售

（一）销售方式
……
（二）销售步骤
……
（三）销售进度
……

五、赞助商选择标准

选择赞助企业时,主要参照以下标准：

资质因素。赞助企业必须是有实力的企业,是行业内的领先企业；发展前景良好,有充足的资金支付赞助费用。

保障因素。能为成功举办奥运会提供充足、先进、可靠的产品、技术或服务。

报价因素。企业所报的赞助价格是选择赞助企业最重要的考虑因素之一。

品牌因素。企业具有良好的社会形象和企业信誉,企业的品牌和形象与奥林匹克理想和北京奥运会的理念相得益彰,产品符合环保标准。

推广因素。企业在市场营销和广告推广方面投入足够的资金和做出其他努力,以充分利用奥运会平台进行市场营销,同时宣传和推广北京2008年奥运会。

第二部分 特许计划

一、奥运会特许计划

奥运会特许经营是指奥组委授权合格企业生产或销售带有奥组委标志、吉祥物等奥林匹克知识产权的产品。为享有这一权利,特许企业将向奥组委交纳一定的特许权费,以此对奥运会做出贡献。

国际会议市场开发 | The Marketing of International Conference

……

二、北京2008年奥运会特许计划

（一）北京2008年奥运会特许计划的宗旨

……

（二）运营模式和发展阶段

……

整个计划由两部分组成：国内计划和国际计划。国内计划将在2003年下半年开始。国际计划在雅典2004年奥运会结束后开始。

……

1. 选择特许企业

在选择特许企业（生产或销售）时，我们将坚持以下原则：

（1）通过市场调查、资质评估、实地考察等方式选择特许企业。

（2）重点考察内容包括资金实力、生产能力、质量管理、设计能力、环保标准、防伪措施、营销策略、销售渠道、物流管理、售后服务等。

（3）特许企业应有相应的财务能力按时交纳特许权费。

（4）采取阶段性签约的模式。合同期满后，要对特许经营商生产和经营情况重新评估，以决定是否续约。

2. 特许权费的收取

对于每个特许企业都将收取入门费和最低保证金。入门费不得抵扣特许权费，最低保证金可抵扣特许权费。

（三）奥运会邮、币计划

1. 奥运会纪念邮票计划

奥运会纪念邮票计划将包括三个具体项目：普通邮票项目、个性化邮票项目和邮品。题材以体育（奥林匹克运动、国际奥委会形象、组委会形象、中国奥委会形象、奥运会项目、火炬接力、开闭幕式等）、文化（中国传统文化，北京传统文化和人文景观）、比赛场馆等内容为主。

整体计划在2003年底开始，时间跨度为5年。

2. 奥运会纪念币计划

奥运会纪念币计划包括纪念币和流通币两个部分，题材以体育（奥林匹克运动、国际奥委会形象、组委会形象、中国奥委会形象、奥运会项目、火炬接力、开闭幕式等）、文化（中国传统文化，北京传统文化和人文景观）、比赛场馆等内容为主。

Analysis and Summary 分析概要

　　该案例选取一个中文国际会议作为样本,较为全面展现了国内举办国际会议的市场开发工作。由该案例可以看出,国内有关单位进行国际会议市场开发时,日益重视赞助商的甄选标准和权益。该案例是国内有关单位举办国际会议时市场开发的大胆尝试,具有代表性。

Questions 思考题

1. 在该案例中,北京奥运会的赞助商和特许计划有几个方面?
2. 在该案例中,国际会议的市场开发与一般国外举办的国际会议时的市场开发有何差异?

2.4 Case Comparison 案例对比

	2008北京奥运会	2015 Italy World Expo
商标		
吉祥物		

国际会议市场开发 | The Marketing of International Conference

上述图片均来自两大活动的官方网站

Analysis and Summary 分析概要

根据国际会议市场开发的基本内容,案例对比将所选择的中文和英文案例分块进行比较,以突显中外进行国际会议市场开发各项工作中的异同。

Questions 思考题

1. 通过上述两个案例的学习,可否明确国际会议市场开发的主要内容?

2. 上述两份国际会议市场开发在主要内容上有何异同？

3. 上述两份国际会议市场开发主要内容有何内在联系？

3. Supplementary Reading
拓展阅读

3.1 Why We Must Protect Rio 2016 Official Brands

> The Olympic and Paralympic brands express the vision and values of the Rio 2016 Games. They are the visual representations of the ideals of the Olympic and Paralympic Movements, in addition to being a valuable marketing property.
>
> To preserve the official brands, guaranteeing their integrity and emotional value is essential for the maintenance and continuity of the Olympic and Paralympic Movements.
>
> The official partners that associate themselves with the Games, mainly due to their belief in the philosophy contained in the Olympic and Paralympic ideals, will add great value to the construction and strengthening of the brands, products and services.
>
> Accordingly, it is extremely important to ensure the partners the right to associate themselves with the Games and preserve the emotional and commercial value of the brands.

From Brand Protection Guidelines — Rio 2016 http://www.rio2016.com/sites/default/files/users/flavio/brand_protection_guideline_for_advertising_market.pdf

Questions and Answers

Directions: In this part there is one question. You need to ask the question based on the words or phrases from the passage.

Why Brazil must protect Rio 2016 official brands?

Blank-filling

Directions: Complete each brackets with appropriate words or phrases from the

passage.

The Olympic and Paralympic brands hold the (　　) of the Rio 2016 Games. They are the visual of the ideals of the Olympic and Paralympic Movements, and also being a valuable marketing property.

3.2 2014南京青奥会

北京时间2010年2月11日(温哥华当地时间10日),在温哥华举行的国际奥委会第122届全会决定,将2014年第二届夏季青年奥林匹克运动会的承办权授予中国的南京市。

以下为南京青奥会市场开发相关事宜

南京青奥会知识产权名录

一、注册商标

    会徽   吉祥物图案

二、特殊标志(6个)

1. 青奥(除第5、11、19、28、31、33类外的39类均已获得特殊标志登记证书)
2. 青奥会(全类)
3. 南京青奥会NANJING YOUTH OLYMPIC GAMES (全类)
4. 2014青奥会 2014 YOUTH OLYMPIC GAMES (全类)
5. 南京2014 Nanjing2014(全类)
6. 吉祥物名称砳砳LELE (1~8, 14, 15, 22~24, 26, 27, 31~40, 43~45类已获得登记)

三、著作权

口号:分享青春　共筑未来(中文、英语、法语、西班牙语、俄语、阿拉伯语六国语言)

倒计时牌

6. 体育图标

射箭 Archery　竞技体操 Artistic Gymnastics　田径 Athletics　羽毛球 Badminton　三人篮球 3X3 Basketball

橄榄球 Rugby　帆船 Sailing　射击 Shooting　游泳 Swimming　乒乓球 Table tennis

曲棍球 Hockey　柔道 Judo　现代五项 Modern Pentathlon　艺术体操 Rhythmic Gymnastics　赛艇 Rowing

沙滩排球 Beach Volleyball　拳击 Boxing　皮划艇 Canoe-Kayak　自行车 Cycling　跳水 Diving

跆拳道 Taekwondo　网球 Tennis　铁人三项 Triathlon　举重 Weightlifting　摔跤 Wrestling

沙滩排球 Beach Volleyball　拳击 Boxing　皮划艇 Canoe-Kayak　自行车 Cycling　跳水 Diving

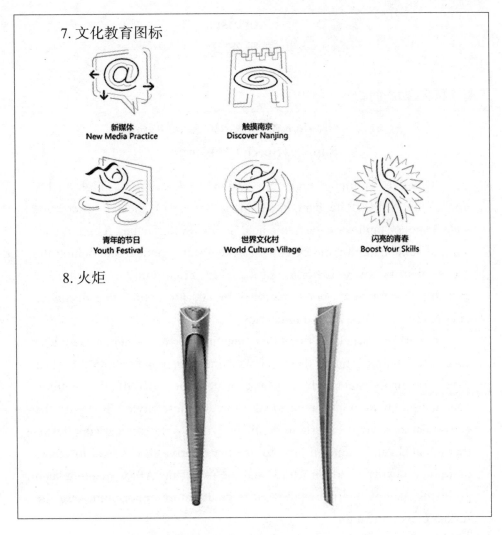

注：上述图片均来自南京青奥会官方网站

问答

1. 结合通过的材料，分析2014年南京青奥会的注册商标和特殊标示的类型。

2. 分析2014年南京青奥会吉祥物设计可能存在的问题。

Exercises
课后练习

1.阅读材料,回答问题。

> ### China's Creative Build APEC State Banquet Supplies Special Tableware
>
> "Creative boutique high-end design lead China's high-quality goods, the APEC state banquet dialogue and 2014 special water cube state banquet tableware tasting" held in the water cube. A number of cultural scholars and industry experts reveal state banquet site behind the scenes, discuss how to better use of the APEC opportunity to promote and industry development, boost national brand, promoting the fusion of culture creativity and related industries.
>
> Remarkable week of the APEC meeting in November in Beijing a successful ending. Among them, the welcoming banquet held in the water cube contains "on good if water, water for all" of the cultural connotation, with multidimensional show Chinese style. In 13 of the conversation, several experts in-depth analytical state banquet supplies of traditional features, and on how to use the creative forces lead to create more high-quality goods in China, and the use of the APEC meeting such problems such as international event to create more opportunities for the further communication.
>
> 21 economies leaders use colorful tableware to let a person shine at the moment. According to introducing, the state banquet boutique realize China creative, design, manufacturing, mainly in "prosperous time" as the design theme, meaning "spanning, ruyi peace." Its core elements "best treasure phase lines" derived from Dunhuang frescoes in the grain, after screening, extracting phase pattern, peony, moire, ruyi lines such as the traditional Chinese auspicious patterns, and then by the designer blend of innovation, extracting core graphics, it used throughout in the design of each product.

国际会议市场开发 | The Marketing of International Conference

> The banquet tableware used colored enamel porcelain technique, the techniques from the late Qing dynasty emperor Kangxi years, represents the highest form of Chinese ceramics production, known as "out of print art palace treasures." On the basis of inheriting ancient skill, tableware also combined with modern stickers technology innovation, realize the "China to create," reflects the new trend of development of modern ceramic technology.

(1) What is the strategy for the tableware market development in this state banquet?

(2) What is the method for the market development of the leaders' suit in the APEC?

2. 阅读下面的材料，回答问题。

怀柔借APEC打造"国际会都"

作为2014年亚太经济合作组织（APEC）领导人非正式会议会场所在地，怀柔自1995年举办世界妇女大会之后，再次成为全世界瞩目的焦点。

从联合国第四次世界妇女大会，到世界小姐、国际小姐中国赛区总决赛、东亚商务论坛，再到如今的APEC会议，这些年来，一系列国际性重要会议及活动纷纷选择在怀柔举办。

漫步在如诗如画的雁栖湖旅游风景区，蓝天流云，青山碧波。在APEC会址核心岛工程建设中，特别注重生态环保。为了不占用鸟类生存空间，建设方在岛上专门设置了3000个鸟舍。

在首都环境资源日益趋紧形势下，近年来怀柔着力转变经济发展方式，推进产业结构调整，构建高端引领、创新驱动、绿色低碳的产业发展模式。

从世妇会到APEC，承接一系列国际性会议活动让怀柔从单纯的

> "山水之城"变为一座"会都"。
>
> 近年来,怀柔在市政建设、环境整治、交通水电、治污减排和旅游升级上加快步伐。仅在环境整治上,就拆除违法建筑近9000处,280多个村庄环境得到美化,私搭乱建、垃圾乱堆、污水横流等现象彻底改观。
>
> APEC会议为怀柔带来了跨越发展的重大机遇。借助此次盛会,这片"怀山柔水"之地将打通会展、文化、科技、旅游、影视等多业态,以生态环保的发展理念与综合性服务,向世界高端会议最佳举办地的目标阔步前行。

(1) 分析材料中怀柔通过APEC会议进行市场开发的经验。

(2) 分析该段材料对于重庆市举办"中国—中东欧国家地方领导人会议"的对外推介作用。

(3) 结合该段材料,借助区域经济发展特性,分析重庆通过国际会议进行市场开发的可行方案。

3. 阅读材料,回答问题。

> The World Economic Forum (WEF) is a Swiss nonprofit foundation, based in Cologny, Geneva. Recognized by the Swiss authorities as the international institution for public-private cooperation, its mission is cited as "committed to improving the state of the world by engaging business, political, academic, and other leaders of society to shape global, regional, and industry agendas."
>
> The Forum is best known for its annual winter meeting in Davos, a mountain resort in Graubünden, in the eastern Alps region of Switzerland. The meeting brings together some 2,500 top business leaders,

国际会议市场开发 | The Marketing of International Conference

international political leaders, selected intellectuals, and journalists to discuss the most pressing issues facing the world. Often this location alone is used to identify meetings, participation, and participants with such phrases as, "a Davos panel" and "a Davos Man."

(1) Please list five world famous sceneries for the international conference.

Country	Scenery	International Conference venue

(2) What is positive influence of the scenery in Davos on the World Economic Forum?

Chapter 7

The Registration of International Conference
国际会议注册

Overview
内容概览

The registration is the act of recording a name or information on an official list. The registration in an international conference is the procedure to collect the personal information of the participants at the host agency. In this way, the host can carry forward to the latter part of the conference. It is one of the fundamental issues for a successful conference.

会议注册是了解参会人员基本信息的有效途径,对于会议的各项安排具有指导性作用;同时注册缴费是会议经费的重要来源和保障;另外注册工作是会议举办者与参与者沟通并传达会议组织工作的最重要环节,因此意义重大。

在进行会议注册工作时,要准备充分,考虑周全,如选择何种注册方式,以及注册时间、地点的选择等,都要求工作人员对会议性质和规模、参会人员基本情况、会议注册工作等较为熟悉,且根据实际情况灵活安排布置。

1. Basic Knowledge
基础知识

1.1 The Meaning of Registration 会议代表注册的意义

The registration is an effective way to collect the basic information of all the attendee in an international conference. It is of great significance for the arrangement of the meeting.

The facets of international conference registration payments are as follows:

国际会议注册 | The Registration of International Conference

(1) Registration fees are an important source of revenue of an international conference. Participants can get important information from the meeting which can provide the participants with rare networking opportunities. Therefore, according to the principle that "You get what you pay for," certain membership dues are reasonable.

(2) Sometimes, conference organizers also specify that part of the charges are used for special purposes, such as funding for low-income participants, or making public welfare undertakings, etc.

(3) Some international conferences, like businesses, often host celebrities, who charge a premium or a registration fee of many of the participants.

(4) All participants and sponsors expect to see a return on the time and money they put into the international meetings.

The meaning of "registration works" is as follow.

(1) Delegates are integral parts of a meeting. The international conference is designed to provide a platform for delegates from different countries, and exchange ideas on a particular field of knowledge. Without the participation of delegates, the meeting will lose its value.

(2) Registration work is the most important way in which organizers and participants communicate.

(3) For international conference, registration fees are one of the important sources for the meeting organization, but the meeting itself can get related funding from donors.

(4) Another important purpose is to collect information to prepare meeting materials and the rational allocation for the conference organizers.

The Meaning of International Conference Registration Payment 国际会议注册缴费的意义

（1）要求与会者缴纳注册费是国际会议取得财政来源的重要方面。国际会议的开支浩大，与会者可以从会上获得重要的信息，会议又为与会者提供了难得的公关机会，因此根据"有取必有付出"的原则，收取一定的与会费是合理的。

（2）有时会议主办者还明确说明部分收费的特殊用途，例如资助低收入者与会、用于某项公益事业等。

（3）有的国际会议也具有商业性质,常以名人出席为号召,收取高额的注册费。

（4）在不景气的经济环境下,制定更加积极的项目和奖励计划才能吸引更多人注册参会。参会人员和赞助商都期望他们投入到国际会议中的时间和金钱能有所回报。

The Meaning of Registration Work 做好会议代表注册工作的意义

（1）会议代表是会议的有机组成部分。国际会议可以为来自不同国家的代表在某一领域的沟通、交流提供平台。没有与会代表的参与,便失去了会议的目标和意义。

（2）会议代表注册工作是会议举办者与会议参与者沟通并传达会议组织工作的最重要环节。

（3）对国际会议来说,参会代表所缴纳的参会注册费是会议组织所需经费的重要来源之一,也关系着会议本身是否能争取到相关专业资助者资金资助。

（4）代表注册的另外一个重要目的在于收集信息,使会议组织者提前掌握参会人员信息,以便准备会议资料、合理配置会议资源。

1.2 Registration Method 代表注册方法

Registration can be divided into the pre-meeting and on-site registration.

(1) Before starting the registration, the first thing is to establish a variety of registration systems, including the registration, the establishment and classification of the registration fee, refund policy, and the early registration deadline as well. For the registration fee, a reasonable one should guarantee that the meeting goes smoothly and should be as low as possible to attract more delegates.

(2) In order to build solid network, the database of the participant was strongly recommended to the organizer.

(3) The conference organizers should not only offer high quality international business services for the representatives, but also arrange convenient transportation, economical hotels, and tourism services for them.

(4) Guests usually informed by the organizers in advance. The basic requirement of the conference should be classified in the invitation. The meeting notice should specify the time and place, bus line, etc.

国际会议注册 | The Registration of International Conference

(5) After sending a circular, one must handle the registration information and take charge of registration fee procedure.

(6) Registration can collect fees so that the conference organizers can follow the latest developments of the meeting, then they can make corresponding adjustments according to the actual situation of the representatives.

The on-site registration process is as follows: taking fees, making nametags for representatives at the scene, giving representatives the best price and related paperwork.

会议代表注册可分为会前注册和现场注册。

The Registration Process Before the Meeting 会前注册流程

（1）在开始注册之前，首先要建立、明确注册相关的各种制度，包括注册的方式、注册费用的制定及分类、退款政策、前期注册截止日期等政策。特别是注册费的设置，合理的注册费应该是既能保证会议各项顺利进行又能尽量降低以吸引更多的代表参加。

（2）政策明确后，开始建立各项数据库，以备查询。

（3）会议组织者不仅能为国际参会代表提供高质量的会务服务，还能为他们安排交通便利、实惠的餐饮、旅游服务。为国际会议参会代表指定大会协议酒店并提供特别报价仍然是会前注册工作中不可缺少的一部分。

（4）制作参会通知。嘉宾通常需要盖有主办单位红章的参会通知，通知可在稿件接收通知时一并发出，最好注明邀请参会，并参与大会交流，这样方便参会代表请假。会前通知要写明时间、地点、乘车路线、现场报道流程等。

（5）发出通知之后，便是处理注册信息，收取注册费的过程。

（6）定期制作报表、包含注册情况、收费情况、使会议组织者了解会议进展，根据参会代表的实际情况做出相应的调整。

The On-site Registration Process 现场注册流程

现场注册流程如下:(1)填写代表注册信息；(2)交费；(3)现场制作代表胸牌；(4)发给代表胸牌等相关票据；(5)领取大会出版物。

1.3 Registry Arrangement 注册处布置

The registry must be visible when guests enter the venue. Generally, it is located to the main entrance.

The layout of the registry can be arranged on the last night; one should prepare two to three hours for the items which require placement and layout. Registry forms, gifts that require registration, and cash counters that require ticket reimbursement, etc.

Registration required items mainly include the room card, paper, calculator, pen and accommodation, dinner list form, participating in cultural activities form, etc. Meeting materials can be put into the guest room in advance.

The formal registry should be set back behind the table, which will not only be convenient for guests to find, but be required for guest registration. The registration table area includes meeting information, gift distribution area, air ticket reimbursement zone, and accommodation zone. The general registration process order is as follows: registering for the meeting — receiving materials — reimbursing flights — receiving accommodation room cards. Registration tables should be covered with red or blue table cloth.

Site Selecting 地点选择

注册处一定要显眼,方便嘉宾一入酒店就能找到会务组,注册处一般设在酒店大厅正对面或左或右,一进酒店或者会展中心就能找到的地方。

Time 布置时间

注册处的布置最好在开始注册前一天晚上开始,准备需要摆放和布置的东西,一般需要两三个小时左右。注册时所需的注册表、礼品、机票报销所需的点钞机等,可在注册当天进行摆放和布置。

Required Items 所需物件

注册时所需物品主要有房卡、点钞机、计算器、签字笔、住宿登记表、参加晚宴名单登记表、参加文艺活动登记表等。会议资料可提前放入嘉宾房间,也可注册时发放。

The Layout of the Registration 注册处的布局

正式的注册处应在注册台后面设置背板,不但方便嘉宾寻找,而且供嘉宾注册时留影所需。一般注册台设注册区、会议资料、礼品发放区、机票报销区和住宿办理区。一般排列顺序是会议注册—领取资料—报销机票—领取住宿。注册台的桌子一般用红色或蓝色的桌布包裹。

国际会议注册 | The Registration of International Conference

2. Case Study
案例分析

2.1 Case Summary 案例概述

本章选取中外两则案例来展现国际会议注册的异同。第一则英文案例展现了国际会议注册的基本规范。第二则中文案例体现出中国举办国际会议时注册的基本操作规范。

2.2 International Conference on Current Developments in Statistical Sciences

Case Guide-Reading 案例导读

This case is based on the registration of Statistical Sciences. With the elements of the registration for this conference, it provides the key procedures and contents about the registration for the reader.

> The theme of the 2-day international conference is Recent Development in Statistical Sciences. The Department of Career and Professional Development Services (CPDS), has decided to sponsor this conference in collaboration with the Carleton University, Canada. Participants are expected to come from all over the world including researchers and academics as well as representatives from business, industry, government bodies and non-government agencies. This conference will cover all areas of theoretical and applied statistics including:
>
> **REGISTRATION INFORMATION**
>   **REGISTRATION FEES:**
>   The non-refundable registration fee for participants based on country of residence:
>
>   Participants from
>   Bangladesh   Taka 4000.00
>   Participants from
>   SAARC countries   USD100.00
>   Participants from

```
                    Registration Form
                  International Conference on
             Recent Development in Statistical Sciences
           North South University, Dhaka, 26-27 December 2008

  Name (Prof/Dr/Mr)

  Occupation:                        Country of Residence:

  Institution:

  Postal Address:

  Tel:
  Fax:
  E-mail:

  [ ] As a presenter     [ ] As a participant only

  Method of payment
      [ ] Bank draft  [ ] Local order    [ ] Cheque
                         (Bangladesh Taka)  (US dollars)

  Signature: _____

  Date: _____

  Please complete and return this form to the Conference Secretariat by airmail, telefax
  or (preferably) via e-mail before 15th November 2008.

  Secretariat
  International Conference on Recent Development in Statistical Sciences 2008
  Dr Abdul Hannan Chowdhury
  Professor, School of Business
  North South University
  12 Kemal Ataturk Ave.
  Banani, Dhaka-1213, Bangladesh
  Tel: 9885611-20 ext: 251 & Dept. CDPS ext: 131
  Fax: 880-02-8823030
  E-mail: hannan@northsouth.edu or nsustatconf@northsouth.edu
  Conference homepage: http://www.sci.usq.edu.au/staff/khans/stat-conf-2008.pdf
```

Other countries   USD200.00

Students   50% off

Each accompanying person pays half of the applicable regular registration fee.

All participants including paper presenters should register by 30 November 2008.

MODE OF PAYMENT

International participants should send the registration fee in US dollars by Demand Draft in favor of North South University and mailed

国际会议注册 | The Registration of International Conference

> to:
>
> **Dr. Abdul Hannan Chowdhury**
>
> Professor, School of Business&
>
> Chair, Executive Committee
>
> North South University
>
> 12 Kemal Ataturk Avenue
>
> Banani C/A, Dhaka 1213
>
> Bangladesh
>
> E-mail: hannan@northsouth.edu or nsustatconf@northsouth.edu
>
> Participants from Bangladesh should pay the registration fee in Bangladesh Taka.
>
> There is no provision of refund of registration fee for cancellation of registration.

Analysis and Summary 分析概要

This case is selected from the registration of Statistical Sciences which indicates the outline of the registration work. In this case, the information on the attendees and registration fees are primary to the organizer. The format can be recognized as the representative of the registration.

Questions 思考题

What is the composition for registration in this conference?

Compared with conference at home, what are the differences in the registration for this conference?

2.3 2014 年第九届中国 LNG 国际会议

Case Guide-Reading 案例导读

本案例选取一个中文国际会议为素材。通过分析此次国际会议注册，读者可以全面了解国内举办国际会议时注册环节的主要步骤和内容。

我国"十二五"能源规划中,发展低碳经济、促进能源的多元化发展、改善能源结构是能源发展规划的重中之重……"2015中国国际LNG峰会"在行业权威机构的领导下,将于2015年4月22日—23日在北京召开,大会为推动行业发展、设备国产化进程和关联技术革新提供广阔交流平台。

主办单位:

广东油气商会广东省石油学会

协办单位:

美国A&S国际工程公司

会议热点话题:

中国LNG的供应与需求

中国主要的LNG进口终端项目的最新进展

……

关于会议:

……

2014中国LNG大会报名表

会务费:

会务费包括CD版大会文件、茶点、午餐、晚餐。

报名日期	个人	三人以上团体
2014年3月26日之前	3500元/人	3200元/人
2014年3月26日之后	3800元/人	3500元/人

会议地点和住宿:

珠海德翰大酒店(地址:广东省珠海市吉大情侣中路)

会议为参会代表争取了优惠房价,标准房460元/间/晚(含早),住宿费自理。

如需订房请尽早填好订房表回传至会务组。

会务咨询:

郑小姐020-×××××××× 　　　曾小姐020-××××××××

国际会议注册 | The Registration of International Conference

叶先生020-×××××××　　许先生020-×××××××

报名方式：

请填妥会议报名表,并通过传真或电邮发回会务组。

传真:020-×××××××,××××××××　　电邮:×××@×××

会议报名表
〈2014年第九届中国LNG国际会议〉

□先生/□女士　姓名:＿＿＿＿＿（英文/拼音）:＿＿＿＿　职务/职称:＿＿＿＿
公司名称:（中文）＿＿＿＿＿＿＿＿＿＿＿＿＿＿＿＿＿＿＿＿＿
　　　　　（英文）＿＿＿＿＿＿＿＿＿＿＿＿＿＿＿＿＿＿＿＿＿
通讯地址:＿＿＿＿＿＿＿＿＿＿＿＿＿＿＿＿＿邮编:＿＿＿＿＿
电话:＿＿＿＿＿＿传真:＿＿＿＿＿＿手机:＿＿＿＿＿
电子邮箱:＿＿＿＿＿＿＿＿＿＿网址:＿＿＿＿＿＿
请注明:本公司已电汇RMB＿＿＿＿＿到指定帐户。

请于会议前将会务费汇至以下账户：
收款单位:广东油气商会
开户银行:××××
帐号:××××

（温馨提示:请在汇款单上注明"LNG国际会议费"）

广州东方国际旅行社有限公司订房表
〈2014年第九届中国LNG国际会议〉

联系人:付小姐、吴小姐
电话:××××　手机:××××　传真:020-××××　E-mail:××××@189.cn

□先生　□女士　姓名:＿＿＿＿＿＿＿＿＿＿
公司名称:＿＿＿＿＿＿＿＿＿＿＿＿＿＿＿
地址:＿＿＿＿＿＿＿＿＿＿＿＿＿＿＿＿＿
手机:＿＿＿＿＿＿＿＿＿电话:＿＿＿＿＿＿
传真:＿＿＿＿＿＿＿＿＿Email:＿＿＿＿＿＿

珠海德翰大酒店　□标准间:460元/间/晚（含早）

入住时间:＿＿＿＿＿＿　离开时间:＿＿＿＿＿＿
房间数:＿＿＿＿＿＿　备注:＿＿＿＿＿＿

（温馨提示:若无定金,预定客房仅保留至当天下午六时正）

（需要开具发票报销的请来电或来邮时提出,否则按照上述流程执行,事后不予以补办）

Analysis and Summary 分析概要

该案例选取一个中文国际会议作为样本,较为全面地展现了国内举办国际会议的会议注册工作。由该案例可以看出,国内有关单位进行国际会议注册时,较为重视参会人员信息和住宿信息的收集。该案例是国内有关单位举办国际会议时会议注册的一般做法。

Questions 思考题

1. 在该案例中,会议注册由哪几个方面组成?
2. 在该案例中,国际会议注册与一般国外举办的国际会议时的注册有何差异?

2.4 Case Comparison 案例对比

会议名称	2014年第九届中国LNG国际会议	International Conference on Recent Development in Statistical Sciences
注册时间	2014年4月9日 14:30 — 20:00	By 30 November 2008
注册地点	德翰大酒店:广东省珠海市吉大情侣中路	Dhaka Sheraton Hotel La Vinci Hotel Sundarban Hotel Hotel Sweet Dream Hotel Sarina
会务费用	会务费包括CD版大会文件、茶点、午餐、晚餐(个人/团体)。	The non-refundable registration fee for participants based on country of residence: Participants from Bangladesh Taka 4000.00 Participants from SAARC countries USD100.00 Participants from Other countries USD200.00 Students 50% off Each accompanying person pays half of the applicable regular registration fee.

国际会议注册 | The Registration of International Conference

注册内容	填写申请、会费汇款、预订酒店	fill in the application form remit fees book hotels

Analysis and Summary 分析概要

根据国际会议注册的基本内容，案例对比将所选择的中文和英文案例分块进行比较，以突显中外进行国际会议注册各项工作中的异同。

Questions 思考题

1. 通过上述两个案例的学习，可否明确国际会议注册的主要工作？
2. 上述两份国际会议注册在主要内容上有何异同？
3. 上述两份国际会议注册的主要内容有何内在联系？

3. Supplementary Reading 拓展阅读

3.1 2015 Harvard Model United Nations Conference

Harvard Model United Nations is a four-day international relations simulation for high school students held annually in downtown Boston. At HMUN, delegates gain insight into the workings of the United Nations and the dynamics of international relations by assuming the roles of UN representatives and members of other international bodies and national cabinets. HMUN is an exciting opportunity for students to debate issues that confront world leaders and to draft resolutions in response to these global issues. Participants will develop their abilities to work with others who are equally motivated and passionate about the topics of debate and to respond to global concerns.

HMUN 2015 builds upon decades of experience. In 1927, Harvard held its first annual Model League of Nations, followed by the first Model United Nations conference in 1953.

This longevity and the dynamic that only a conference of a size can provide make HMUN the preeminent simulation of its kind in the world.

> True to the spirit of the United Nations, founded in 1945, HMUN strives to foster a constructive forum for open dialogue on complex global issues, including international peace and security and economic and social progress. HMUN stresses the in-depth examination and resolution of pressing issues, emphasizing process over product. During the conference, students learn the importance of balancing national interests with the needs of the international community, while also learning about the powers and limitations of international negotiation. Delegates will preserve their countries' national policy while negotiating in the face of other, sometimes conflicting, international policies.
>
> According to the participants from China Mainland, the organizers of Harvard Model United Nations regarded Taiwan as a sovereign state in the official paper, which caused the participants protest.

Blank-filling

Directions: Complete each brackets with appropriate words or phrases from the passage.

Harvard Model United Nations is a four-day international relations simulation for high school students. At HMUN, (   ) gain insight into the workings of the United Nations and the dynamics of international relations. HMUN is an exciting opportunity for students to issues that confront world leaders and to draft resolutions to these global issues. (   ) will develop their abilities to work with others to respond to global concerns.

Questions and Answers

Directions: In this part there is one question. You need to answer the question based on the words or phrases from the passage.

What is the major problem for the registration of Harvard Model United Nations?

国际会议注册 | The Registration of International Conference

3.2 国外国际会议注册费

在国际会议中,一般需要参会者缴纳一定数额的注册费。但当中国有关方面参与国际会议时,所发生的注册费在事后的报销过程中将会产生诸多问题。阅读随后国内某高校财务部门关于国际会议注册费的报销规定。

缴纳国外国际会议注册费、论文版面费等可通过学校财务处办理支付手续,使用学校学术交流用汇额度,通过中国银行付款,详见《国际会议注册费等购汇申请及报销流程图》(见学校财务处网页——服务指南)。

因特殊原因未通过学校购汇付款的,报销时的流程如下:

(1) 通过银行汇款:提供报销票据(英文标识 invoice 或 receipt),及相应的银行汇款单据报销。

(2) 网上支付:提供发票或收据(英文标识 invoice 或 receipt),必须同时出具已付款的有效单据,(如信用卡付款账单或信用卡刷卡交易签字小票原件或银行交易回单原件等辅助证明)方能报销。

(3) 国外国际会议注册费、论文版面费付款一律刷卡或汇款。尽量不使用现钞支付。特殊情况,提供发票原件并注明"现金"字样。

所提供的辅助证明如没有外汇汇率比价,为提高工作效率,请在中国银行 http://www.boc.cn/或中国工商银行 http://www.icbc.com.cn/icbc/"外汇牌价"栏目,按发票付款日期查询对应币种外汇牌价并打印作为辅助证明一并提供。

问答题

结合上述材料,思考为何中国有关方面参与国际会议一般均希望外方提供邀请函、发票、获奖证明等纸质文件。

Exercises
课后练习

1. International Conference of Historical Geographers 2015

> 5—10 July 2015, at the Royal Geographical Society (with The Institute of British Geographers) in London, United Kingdom.
>
> How to register http://www.ichg2015.org/registration/travel-information/ -_blank Visit www.ichg2015.eventbrite.com to register.
>
> **Step One:**
>
> Select your registration fee category: "Standard," "Student, retired or unwaged" or "One day." Add "Accompanying Guest" if applicable (accompany guests may only be added alongside another registration fee category).
>
> - Read more about registration fee categories, and what registration includes.
> - Each booking should be for one delegate, plus any accompanying guest directly related to the delegate. The Accompanying Guest fee category may only be used where a booking is made in one of the main fee categories ("Standard" "Student, retired or unwaged" or "One day"). Accompanying Guests may not appear on the conference programme.
> - The organizers will contact attendees booking for one day to confirm the day of attendance. This is likely to happen after the conference programme is confirmed as final. If you need to make firm travel plans, please contact the organizers for advice.
>
> **Step Two:**
>
> Add conference dinner (optional)
> - The conference dinner will be a two-course standing buffet dinner taking place on the evening of Thursday 9 July 2015. The dinner cost includes wine on arrival and with dinner; there will also be a cash bar available. Special diets can be catered for.

国际会议注册 | The Registration of International Conference

Step Three:

Add mid-conference study-visit/field trip (optional) — bookings have now closed.

- Read about mid-conference study visits.
- Please select one trip per person booked, for a maximum of two trips per booking.
- If your accompanying guest will attend a different field trip to the main attendees, please make a note in the space allowed under each attendee's booking to specify which field trip they will attend.

Step Four:

Add post-conference field trip (optional) — bookings have now closed.

- Read more about post-conference field trips.
- Please select one trip per person booked, for a maximum of two places on one trip.

Once you have made all your selections, click Register to continue to the next step.

Step Five:

Check your selections. The box at the top of the page will show what you selected on the previous page. Click Back on your browser to modify if necessary.

Step Six:

Enter the payment information (name, credit/debit card information, and billing address for the person paying for the registration).

- All bookings must be paid in full using a valid credit/debit card at the time of booking. Bookings cannot be confirmed without payment. The organizers regret that they cannot issue invoices for registration, nor can payment be made by other methods.

Step Seven:

Complete attendee information (name, affiliation and other

> information for the person/s attending the conference.
> - Please complete all questions in full.
> - There is space in the booking form to add notes to the organizers with any special requests (dietary, access or otherwise) or to request further information.
>
> **Step Eight:**
>   Complete your booking.
> - A confirmation of booking and PDF receipt will be sent by email when booking is successfully completed.

Questions and Answers

Directions: In this part there are two questions. You need to answer the question based on the words or phrases from the passage.

What is the possible problem for the attendees in this registration procedure?

How can the organizer improve the quality of the registration?

2. 阅读材料，回答问题。

> **2014天津夏季达沃斯参会报名踊跃　注册人数已超千人**
>
> 　　第八届新领军者年会（即2014天津夏季达沃斯论坛）参会代表注册工作目前正有序开展，注册资料显示本届论坛参会代表报名更为踊跃，特别是国际工商界领袖、全球青年领袖、专家学者、媒体领袖等参会人数较2012年均有所增长。据统计，截至7月4日，共有来自88个国家和地区的1003名代表注册出席本届年会，比2012年同期增长32%。
>
> 　　在已注册参会代表中，法国赛诺菲集团、瑞士ABB集团、法国道达尔集团、美国3M公司、美国摩根士丹利、荷兰皇家飞利浦公司等世界500强企业CEO新增注册参会；哈佛大学、卡内基梅隆大学、斯坦福大

国际会议注册｜The Registration of International Conference

> 学、牛津大学、哥伦比亚大学、新加坡国立大学、清华大学、北京大学等国内外著名高校专家学者以及英国广播公司（BBC）、纽约时报、金融时报、消费者新闻与商业频道（CNBC）、法新社（AFP）、中央电视台等国内外媒体代表也已纷纷注册参会。
>
> 　　历届夏季达沃斯论坛的成功举办，扩大了天津的影响力，国际工商界领袖、专家学者等各国嘉宾更为关注天津、关注中国。

（1）根据材料，分析2014天津夏季达沃斯论坛注册人数的特点。

（2）在瑞士召开的冬季达沃斯论坛盛况空前，在业内享有盛誉。而近年在中国举行的夏季达沃斯论坛也热闹非凡。根据所学知识，分析为何作为后起之秀的夏季达沃斯论坛注册人数会年年攀升。

3. 阅读下列三份国际会议注册表，回答问题。

中国国际语言服务业大会会议注册表

单位名称				电邮	
通讯地址				邮编	
是否为中国译协理事或理事单位			会员编号		
是否为中国译协会员或会员单位			会员编号		
联系人		电话		传真	
参会者姓名		性别	职务	手机	
				电邮	
参会者姓名		性别	职务	手机	
				电邮	
参会者姓名		性别	职务	手机	
				电邮	

拟交费用	早报名(9月30日前)(以注册费到账时间为准) 中国译协理事和理事单位工作人员：人(1500元/人注册费) 中国译协会员和会员单位工作人员：人(1800元/人注册费) 非中国译协会员：人(3000元/人注册费) 高等院校教师代表： 人(1000元/人注册费) 共计费用：
	正常报名(10月20日前)(以注册费到账时间为准) 中国译协理事和理事单位工作人员：人(1800元/人注册费) 中国译协会员和会员单位工作人员：人(2200元/人注册费) 非中国译协会员：人(3500元/人注册费) 高等院校教师代表： 人(1300元/人注册费) 共计费用：
注册费 汇款方式	户名：中国翻译协会 开户行：中国工商银行北京百万庄支行 账号：×××× 汇款注明：会议注册费

注意事项：

请将填好的注册表邮件回复至event××@tac-online.org.cn。

注册工作联系人及电话：罗×× 010-68329××　　李×× 010-68997××

传真：010-6899×× 68990××　　电子信箱：event××@tac-online.org.cn

(1) 上述国际会议注册表有缺陷？如果有缺陷，请指出。

(2) 如果上述国际会议注册表有缺陷，请提出合理修改意见。

The On-site Service of International Conference
国际会议会场服务

Overview
内容概览

A well-coordinated venue service is a grantee that international meetings run smoothly and come to a successful conclusion. The purpose of convening an international conference is to exchange information and develop ideas. Therefore, the on-site service is significant for international conference.

国际会议会场服务工作的协调有序,有助于国际会议顺利进行并取得圆满成功。召开国际会议的目的是交流思想、沟通信息、开发创意、联络感情、扩大交往,因此,搞好国际会议的现场服务意义重大。

1. Basic Knowledge
基础知识

1.1 Guests Guide and Check-in 嘉宾引领和签到

Guests guide include two parts: preparation work before the guest arrival, and some certain guide actions. Preparation work mainly includes placing directional signs in strategic areas such as lift entrances, stair entrances, street crossings, etc. Certain guide actions include guiding important guests and normal guests. The check-in produces timely and accurate statistics about the number of attendees, which will benefit the arrangement of the conference. For some conferences, the organizer imposes minimal constrain for the attendees, otherwise, the conferences will be invalid. Therefore, check-in for international conference is an important pre-conference work, it should be carefully prepared, well organized, and have timely statistics.

Guests Guide 嘉宾引领

嘉宾的引领包括两个部分：一是引领前的准备工作，二是引领的具体过程。引领前的工作主要是设置相应的指示牌，需要指示牌的地方主要有电梯口、楼梯口、道路转角处等。引领的具体过程包括重要嘉宾的引领和一般嘉宾的引领。

Check-in 嘉宾签到

会议签到就是为了及时准确地统计到会人数，以便于安排会务工作，有些会议只有达到一定人数才能召开，否则会议通过的决议无效。因此会议签到是一项重要的会前工作。签到包括会议嘉宾的签到、会议观众的签到和媒体的签到。

常见的签到方式有：簿式签到、卡片签到、会议工作人员代为签到、座次表签到、计算机签到。签到工作要认真准备、有序组织、及时统计。

1.2 Tea Break 茶歇

Tea Break refers to a snack taken during a break in the work day. As with the international conference, tea break has special function, and is an essential part of the conference, providing all participants with the chance to converse freely and get to know each other more deeply.

茶点，虽然看起来只是一天膳食中的小部分，和整个会议比起来更微不足道，但是，如果安排合理、点心单处理得当，它可以成为整天或整个会议的亮点。茶歇安排有两大要素，一个是时间，另一个是地点。

Tea Time 茶歇时间

一天中最好安排至少两次茶歇，一次在早餐与午餐之间，一次在午餐与晚餐之间。

Tea Place 茶歇地点

茶歇地点的选择取决于与会者的数量。休憩地点不一定集中于某个场所。与会者数量众多时，可能需安排几个地点作为小憩的场所。

如果会议的目的之一是加强与会者之间的沟通，扩大他们的交际圈，那么就要设计一个中心休憩区，周围连带几个小的休憩点，这样，所有的与会者都会在休息时间集中到这一区域，增加了交流的机会。如果会议的主要

国际会议会场服务 | The On-site Service of International Conference

目标不是扩大人际交往,或者休息的时间非常短,与会者又众多,那么把小憩的地点选在分会议室旁会是个不错的选择。场所内要有路标指示并安排有服务员引导与会人员至最近的休息室。

1.3 Conference Hall Arrangement 会场布置

The conference room layout is quite important to the international conference. Here are a few of the popular examples of layouts. Cabaret style is the most popular, with up to 6 delegates seated around a round table all facing forward. Boardroom layout can be set as a solid table or for a larger number of delegates an open square. Theatre layout is normally set out with a stage and 2 side isles. U-Shape is ideal for small numbers of delegates. The classroom layout is mainly used when an exam will take place at the end of the session.

不同性质的会议,要求有不同的会场设计原则与形式进行会场设计时注意会场色调的协调,与会议的类型和主题相适应。

1.3.1 会场整体布局的要求 the Requirements of the Overall Layout of Venue

(1) 庄重、美观、舒适,体现出会议主题和气氛,同时还要考虑会议的性质、规格、规模等因素。

(2) 会场的整体格局要根据会议的性质和形式创造出和谐的氛围。

(3) 中大型会议要保证一个绝对的中心,因此多采用半圆形,大小方形的形式,以突出主持人和发言人。

(4) 小型会场要注意集中和方便。

1.3.2 会场布置的基本原则 the Basic Principles of Venue

(1) 切合会议主题 In Line with the Theme。

会场布置要切合会议主题,要与会议的中心内容相一致。有的会议要求气氛热烈,有的会议要求简洁明快,有的会议要求庄严肃穆。

(2) 区别会议类型 Difference Between Conference Type。

会场布置要与会议的类型吻合。不同性质的会议,对会场的功能有不同的要求。一切从会议要达到的效果出发,会议需要哪些功能,会场布置就突出哪些功能。

(3) 追求整体协调 The Pursuit of the Overall Coordination。

第一,色彩协调。会场的色彩要协调,如墙壁的颜色、桌椅的颜色、幕布

157

的颜色、会标的颜色等,要协调一致。第二,大小适中。会场内物品,如会标、旗子、音响设备等要大小适中。第三,物品相宜。会议桌上摆放的物品要与会议的性质相符,如座谈会、茶话会等可适当摆放一些水果、瓜子、糖果、矿泉水等,而一般的会议只宜摆一些茶水,或只在主席台上摆放茶水。

1.3.3 会场布局 The Venue Layout

会场的格局要根据会议场地条件和会议的进行方式来决定。一般会场的格局有以下几种。

(1) 剧院式 Theater。

它是在会议厅内面向讲台摆放一排陪座椅,中间留有较宽的过道。其特点是:在留有过道的情况下,最大程度地摆放座椅,最大限度地将空间利用起来,在有限的空间里可以保证最大限度的容纳人数。

(2) 课桌形 Classroom Shape。

按教室式布置会议室,每个座位的空间会根据桌子的大小而有所不同。其特点是:安排布置时有一定的灵活性;参加会议者可有放置资料及记笔记的桌子;可以最大限度地容纳人数。教室式布局适合各类讲座。

(3) U字形 U-shape。

将桌子连接摆放成长方形,在长方形的前方开口,椅子摆放在桌子外围。通常开口处摆放放置投影仪的桌子,中间会放置植物以做装饰。这种布局方式的特点是:不设主持会议人的位置,可以营造比较放松的氛围;可摆放几个麦克风以便自由发言。马蹄形布局适合展示、研讨等类型的会议。

(4) 圆形或椭圆形 Round or Oval。

这种方式是在房间内放置一些圆形或椭圆形的桌子,椅子围绕着桌子摆放,以便所有观众都面向前方。其特点是:不突出主席的重要性,注重与会者平等,鼓励与会者之间进行讨论。这种布局方式适合于各类讨论会。国际会议常用圆桌方式布局。

(5) 回字形 Rectangle Shape。

将会议室内摆放的桌子摆放成中空方形,不留缺口,椅子摆在桌子外围。中空方形式会场安排主持人的位置,可分别在不同位置摆放麦克风,以便不同位置的参会者发言。采用此种方式布局会场容纳人数较少,对会议空间有一定的要求。中空方形式会场常用于学术讨论会、座谈会等类型的会议。

国际会议会场服务 | The On-site Service of International Conference

1.4 The Venue Management Work 会场管理工作

A venue manager is the person who is in charge of the venue, which may be a hall, theatre, conference centre, or hotel. Their main job is to oversee activities and guarantee that the facilities are clean and stand by. Stage personnel have to work with the venue manager. Designers can obtain copies of the stage plans from the venue manager.

The following skills needed: experience with technical events, financial management experience, excellent communication, highly developed administrative and organizational capability.

Playing PPT 播放 PPT

负责播放流程 ppt 的人员要对嘉宾、主持人有深入的了解，熟记会议流程，依照流程播放 ppt。播放音乐时，需要与音响管理人员密切联系，保证音乐质量，营造合适的会议氛围。

Guest Speaker Time Control 控制嘉宾演讲时间

每一场会议都有一定的时间安排，对嘉宾的发言时间有一定限制。从嘉宾开始发言时计时，规定时间快到时，可适当提醒，引起演讲者的注意。

Maintaining the Order of the Venue 维护会场秩序

在会议进行期间，工作人员应分散在会场各个区域，负责维持本区域的秩序。

Microphone Management 话筒管理

国际会议上一般会设置互动环节，以便嘉宾与观众进行互动，这就需要专门的工作人员为观众提供话筒。

Photo 合影留念

会议结束之后，要组织各领导嘉宾合影留念。拍照时一定要事先制定好拍照的座次表，保证拍照有条不紊地进行。

2. Case Study
案例分析

2.1 Case Summary 案例概述

本章选取中外两则案例来展现国际会场服务的异同。第一则英文案例展现了国外国际会议会场服务的基本内容和规范。第二则中文案例体现出中国举办国际会议时会场服务的基本内容和操作规范。

2.2 2015 Tokyo International Anime Fair

Case Guide-Reading 案例导读

This case is based on the venue service of Tokyo International Anime Fair. With the elements of the on-site service, it examines the key procedures and contents about the venue service for the reader.

> The Tokyo International Anime Fair also known as Tokyo International Animation Fair was one of the largest anime trade fairs in the world, held annually in Tokyo, Japan. The first event was held in 2002 as "Tokyo International Anime Fair 21". The event was held at Tokyo Big Sight, a convention and exhibition center in Tokyo Bay, in late March. Usually, the first one or two days of the fair were weekdays and the entrance was open only to industry members and the press; the last two days were scheduled on the weekend and the fair was open to the public.
>
> Besides being an international trade fair, the TAF included related events such as business symposia and other events. Notably, the Tokyo Anime Awards were given for domestic and foreign creations and creators in the event with the name of the event. The event was supported by the Bureau of Industrial and Labor Affairs of Tokyo. Although the event did not have a long history, it and its prizes were recognized in the industry. In 2014, it was merged with the Anime Contents Expo to form AnimeJapan.

国际会议会场服务 | The On-site Service of International Conference

Access to Venue

Route from Principal Stations

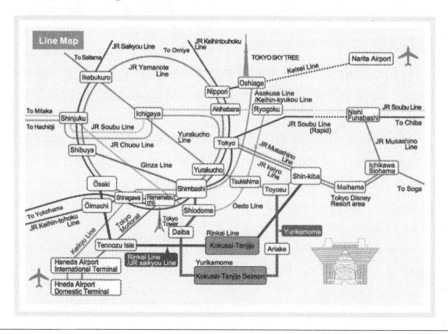

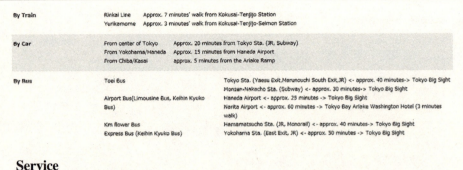

Service

Floor Map

In AnimeJapan 2015, lots of anime related companies and groups that represent Japan exhibit such as unique booth and a variety of contents to this event.

Moreover, many attractive programs by promoter that are advanced than last time are planned and Family Area (part of East Exhibition Halls 6) and Business Area (Reception Hall of Conference Tower, 1F) are established from this time to ensure the satisfaction for general anime fans, business visitors, and all domestic and overseas visitors.

Exhibition groups and products of AnimeJapan 2015 are greater than AnimeJapan 2014.

* Images from the homepage of the conference

国际会议会场服务 | The On-site Service of International Conference

Analysis and Summary 分析概要

This case is selected from the venue service of 2015 Tokyo International Anime Fair which indicates the outline of on-site service. In this case, the information on agenda, venue layout of the conference as well as the route to the venue are carefully prepared by the organizer. This case can be recognized as the representative of the venue service.

Questions 思考题

What is the composition for venue service in this conference?

Compared with conferences at home, what are the differences in the venue service for this conference?

2.3 第九届中国(北京)国际园林博览会

Case Guide-Reading 案例导读

本文属于一则有关国际会议会场服务的中文案例。在该案例中较为详细地阐述了国际会议举办时的诸多信息。通过对本案例的学习，读者可以较为直观和全面地掌握国内举办国际会议时会场服务的基本内容。

> 北京园博会于5月18日开幕，届时128个精品展园将对公众开放，园博会会期长达6个月，直至11月18日闭幕。这是继奥运会之后，首都北京举办的一次历时最长、规模最大的国家级、国际性盛会。
> ……
> 北京园博园是在建筑垃圾填埋场上建设的园林，位于永定河绿色生态发展带的核心区域；是北京市城南行动计划和推进城市西部地区转型升级的重点项目。它的建设和举办是推进丰台永定河绿色生态发展带建设的重要抓手，它对改善生态和投资环境，带动沿岸开发建设和产业升级具有深远意义。……
>
> **服务设施**
> 园博园位于丰台区长辛店镇境内，北至莲石西路，南到梅市口路西延，西至规划北宫路，西南接园博大道，东临永定河新右堤。整个园区呈西北—东南走向，地形狭长：南北长5公里，东西最宽处800米，最

163

窄处只有260米左右。

为方便游客游览,园博园内开设了6大门区供游客出入,并配置了99辆电瓶车。6大门区共有入园闸机124个,出园闸机33个,通行速度为每3秒一个人。紧邻P4停车场的3号门区是主门区,远看状如恐龙的大门格外显眼,进去右手就是主展馆。园内还设置了11个服务区、14个游客服务中心、2个物品寄存处、5个物品租赁中心和3个医疗室。

游客服务中心分布在6个门区和8个服务区之中,可以提供咨询、投诉、广播找人和失物招领等服务。物品寄存处在2号门区和6号门区各有一个。5个物品租赁中心分别在3号、4号、6号门区和1号、9号服务区,有轮椅、婴儿车等设备对外出租,还提供自助导览、导游讲解等有偿服务。医疗室在1号、9号、11号服务区各有一个。

园内共有固定厕位681个,临时厕位150个,无障碍厕位17个。其中,男女固定厕位蹲位为117:341,约为1:2.9。园博园陆地面积267公顷,接近颐和园,由于面积较大,园中引进了无尾气无噪音的观光电瓶车99辆,每辆可乘坐13人,票价30元,游客可凭票乘坐5次。电瓶车的行驶线路为中轴—河堤、中轴—热气球主题园两条。涵盖园内主要景点,游客可就近下车。电瓶车的发车时间和间隔将根据客流量的饱和度由中心统一调度。

27个餐饮区5000座位,1.3万名志愿者微笑服务,园博园中已确定设有27个餐饮服务区,13个特许商品销售店。餐饮方面,确定了包括肯德基、永和大王、和合谷、嘉和一品粥等在内的18个品牌餐饮企业,座位数约5000个,可满足5000人同时就餐。品种包括快餐、冰激凌、烤肉等。其中,园食汇是特为本次园博会开设的餐饮服务店,也是园博园中规模最大的餐饮服务点,位于4号门附近的5号服务区,店内面积800多平方米,可同时容纳500人就餐。园食汇提供70多种中外特色美食。包括冷饮系列、酒水系列、糕点系列、西式简餐系列、中式民族美食系列等。

园博服务

国际会议会场服务 | The On-site Service of International Conference

在线服务

- 北京园博会面积有多大？
- 园博会举办频率？
- 北京园博会志愿者服装什么样？
- 园博会的特色是什么？
- 园博会在什么时间开幕？

*图片来自第九届中国(北京)国际园林博览会主页

Analysis and Summary 分析概要

该案例选取一个中文国际会议作为样本，较为全面地展现了国内举办国际会议的会场服务工作。由该案例可以看出，国内有关单位进行国际会议会场服务时，较为重视会议地址、会场信息电子化、线上线下互动等内容。该案例是国内有关单位举办国际会议时会场服务的基本内容，具有一定的代表性。

Questions 思考题

1. 在该案例中，会场服务由哪几个方面组成？呈现何种特色？
2. 在该案例中，国际会议会场服务与一般国外举办的国际会议的会场服务有何差异？

国际会议会场服务 | The On-site Service of International Conference

2.4 Case Comparison 案例对比

会议名称	第九届中国(北京)国际园林博览会	2015 Tokyo InternationalAnime Fair
服务设施	6大门区、99辆电瓶车、入园闸机124个、出园闸机33个。 11个服务区、14个游客服务中心、2个物品寄存处、5个物品租赁中心和3个医疗室。 园内共有固定厕位681个,临时厕位150个,无障碍厕位17个。 27个餐饮区5000座位,1.3万志愿者微笑服务,13个特许商品销售店。	
网络服务		
服务人员	1.3万志愿者	Unknown

Analysis and Summary 分析概要

根据国际会议会场服务的基本内容,案例对比将所选择的中文和英文案例分块进行比较,以突显中外进行国际会议会场服务各项工作中的异同。

Questions 思考题

1. 通过上述两个案例的学习,可否明确国际会议会场服务的主要工作?
2. 上述两份国际会议会场服务在主要内容上有何异同?
3. 上述两份国际会议会场服务的主要内容有何内在联系?

3. Supplementary Reading
拓展阅读

3.1 2010 G20 Seoul Summit

The 2010 G20 Seoul Summit was the fifth meeting of the G20 heads of government, to discuss the global financial system and the world economy, which took place in Seoul, South Korea, on November 11—12, 2010. Korea was the first non-G8 nation to host a G20 Leaders Summit.

The G20 is the premier forum for discussing, planning, and monitoring international economic cooperation.

The theme of the summit was "Shared Growth Beyond Crisis."

Agenda

The summit leaders addressed several mid- and long-term policy issues, including

Ensuring global economic recovery

Framework for strong, sustainable, and balanced global growth

Strengthening the international financial regulatory system

Modernizing the international financial institutions

Global financial safety nets

Development issues

The risk of a currency war

Representatives met in advance of the leaders' summit. These

国际会议会场服务 | The On-site Service of International Conference

> sherpas were tasked to draft a closing statement for the summit. The debate over currency exchange rates and imbalances was reported to have been "heated."
>
> The Australian Gillard mistaken for Austrian. The figurine of Gillard, dressed in a Sound of Music-style red and white puff-sleeved dress and pink apron, was part of a display of dolls representing leaders attending this week's Group of 20 summit in the city.

Blank-filling

Directions: Complete each brackets with appropriate words or phrases from the passage.

The 2010 G20 Seoul Summit was the fifth meeting of the G20 heads of government, to discuss the global (　　), which took place in Seoul, South Korea, on November 11—12, 2010. Korea was the first non-G8 nation to (　　) a G20 Leaders Summit. This conference is the most important for discussing, planning, and monitoring international economic cooperation.

Questions and Answers

Directions: In this part there is one question. You need to answer the question based on the words or phrases from the passage.
What is the problem for the G20 Seoul Summit on this article?

3.2 国际会议翻译

> 同声传译（Simultaneous interpretation），简称"同传"，又称"同声翻译""同步口译"，是指译员坐在位于会场后方的小屋子（Booth）里，在接受讲话者信息的同时，又将内容通过专用的设备同时口译给听众的一种翻译方式。它适用于参会者来源于不同语种国家的大型国际会议。
>
> 由于该项工作的工作量较大，通常国际会议由两到三名译员轮流进行。因为同声传译效率高，能保证会议的高效进行。当前，绝大多数国际会议均采用同声传译的方式进行。
>
> 第二次世界大战结束后，设在德国的纽伦堡国际军事法庭在审判

法西斯战犯时,首次采用同声传译,这是世界上首次在国际会议中采用同声传译。

　　同声传译员一般收入较高,但是成为同声传译的要求也极为苛刻。译员需要有扎实的语言基础,同时具备广博的知识和良好的学习能力,在每次国际会议前,要进行大量的准备工作。不仅如此,因为其高强度的工作特性,一般译员很难终生从事该项工作,属于青春色彩的职业。

问答

　　阅读材料,思考同声传译译员对于国际会议顺利举办的意义。

举例

　　结合材料,试从新中国成立后的历史中,寻找具有较大影响的译员及其轶事。

Exercises
课后练习

1. 阅读材料,回答问题。

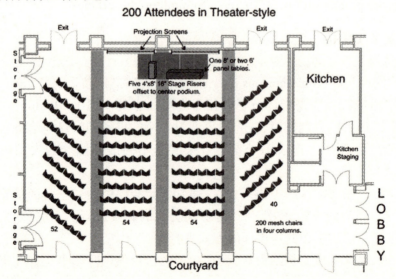

国际会议会场服务 | The On-site Service of International Conference

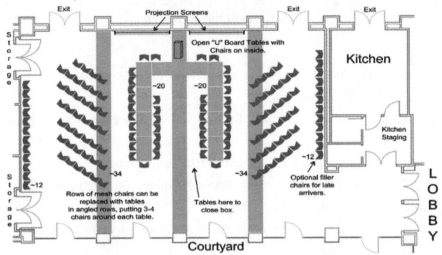

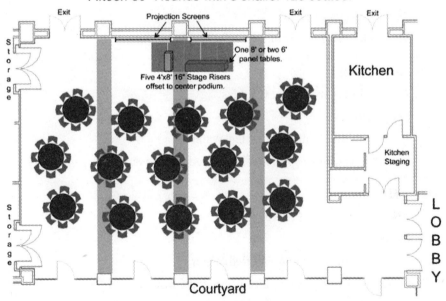

Decision Making

What is the favourite choice for a 100 academic conference? And what is the reason for this decision?

2. 阅读下面由老年人参加的国际联谊会的茶歇安排，回答问题。

Afternoon Snack Break

A La Carte

 Assorted Soft Drinks — Pitchers of Soda & Diet Soda

 Bottles of Soda & Water

 Coffee Service — Freshly Brewed Coffee, Decaffeinated Coffee & Tea

 Coffee Refresh — Coffee Refresh after Initial Service

 Beverage Break — Freshly Brewed Coffee, Decaffeinated Coffee, Tea & Assorted Soft Drinks

 Coffee & Danish — Freshly Brewed Coffee, Decaffeinated Coffee, Tea & Assorted Danish

 Urn of Coffee

 Red Bull Energy Drink

 Starbuck's Double Shot

Chocolate Lovers

 Assorted Freshly Baked Cookies

 Fudge Brownies

 Assorted Soft Drinks & Bottled Water

 Freshly Brewed Coffee, Decaffeinated Coffee & Tea

Heart Healthy

 Cheese, Fresh Fruit & Vegetable Display

 Granola Bars

 Assorted Soft Drinks & Bottled Water

 Freshly Brewed Coffee, Decaffeinated Coffee & Tea

Taste of Philly

 Tasty Cakes

 Philly Soft Pretzels with Mustard

 Italian Water Ice

 Assorted Soft Drinks & Bottled Water

国际会议会场服务 | The On-site Service of International Conference

> Freshly Brewed Coffee, Decaffeinated Coffee & Tea
>
> **Movie Madness**
>
> Assorted Mini Chocolates
>
> Cracker Jacks, Popcorn &Twizzlers
>
> Assorted Soft Drinks & Bottled Water
>
> Freshly Brewed Coffee, Decaffeinated Coffee & Tea

According to the menu of the afternoon snack break, which part do you think is inappropriate?

The Venue Selection of International Conference
国际会议会场保障

Overview
内容概览

When choosing a conference venue, organizer accounts for many things. Whether conference is successfully managed, it was highly depended by the destination, host hotel, and venue. The candidate list, background investigation and field work are the process of venue selection. The cozy physical setting, colorful entertainment, diversified shopping, multiple recreation and tours for delegates are critical for the conference venue.

会场直接关系到会议的质量和效果,选择合适的会场是会议成功的一个基本保障。筹划者在选择会议场所时需要考虑会场大小、会场地点及会场附属设施等因素。选择会议地址有以下四个步骤:初步筛选确定候选名单、背景调查、实地考察、最终选择。大规模的国际会议对其会场有严格要求,国际会议选择会场时需结合会议本身及有关国家、城市等实际情况综合考虑。

1. Basic Knowledge
基础知识

1.1 The Venue Selection Criteria 会场选择的标准

If the venue is too large, and the number of attendees was rare, which will leave too many empty seats and make the participants feel unimportant; if the venue is too small, the attendees will feel crowded, and also can't have a good meeting.

国际会议会场保障 | The Venue Selection of International Conference

When convening meetings lasting one or two hours, the organizers should decide on a venue where participants can stay relatively concentrated; When the meeting lasts more than one day, the venue should be near the residence of the participants.

The venue should be fully equipped with lighting, ventilation, sanitation, service, telephone, address, audio, and other equipment. For all the accessory equipment should be checked carefully.

The Size Should Be Appropriate 大小要适中

会场太大,人数太少,空座太多,松松散散,会给与会人员一种不景气的感觉;会场太小,人数过多,挤在一起,不仅显得小气,也影响会议质量。

The Site Should Be Reasonable 地点要合理

临时召集的会议,一两个小时即散的,要考虑把会场定在与会人员较集中的地方;超过一天的会议,会场要尽可能在与会者住所附近,避免与会者劳碌奔波。

The Affiliated Facilities Should Be Complete 附属设施要齐全

会场的照明、通风、卫生、电话、扩音、录音等各种设备都要配备齐全。对所有附属设备,会务人员要逐一进行检查。不负责的态度很可能会给会议造成损失。

1.2 Venue Selection Steps 会场选择的步骤

When deciding to host a conference, event organizers should select regions and cities first, and then to the venues and facilities. According to the different requirements of the meeting, people will make different choices. Generally, selecting the would-be venue has four steps.

First, organizer needs to make a selection, namely based on meeting objectives, to determine the choice of venue. If the host is a large exhibition, then the choice is quite simple: one can choose meeting hotels or conference and exhibition centers. If one of the goals is simply to have the meeting, a meeting hotel that has many conference rooms is better than a resort hotel, because the latter distracts participants with too many activities and attractions.

It is best to gradually narrow the scope of candidates, and then the candidate list should be submitted to the commission or group discussion to make a final decision. One should not sign the agreement too hastily.

Before deciding on the final location, one should take the time to visit it. While the organizer can obtain space information through the mail, internet, the tourism administrative department or other ways, personal experience is the best option in determining a final selection of a venue.

When narrowing down the field of potential candidates, the organizer should get in touch with the location as soon as possible.

举办会议首先要选择地区和城市,然后选择场馆和设施。根据会议要求的不同,人们会做出不同的选择。一般来说,选择会议地址有四个步骤。

Initial Screening to Determine the Candidate List 初步筛选确定候选名单

首先需要做出筛选,即根据会议的目标来确定选择目标。如果举办的是大型展览,那么选择就相对简单,可以选择会议酒店或会展中心。如果目标之一是召开会议,那么拥有众多会议室的会议酒店就比度假区酒店合适,因为度假区酒店里让与会者分心的活动和地点太多。

Background Investigation 背景调查

最好逐渐地缩小候选范围,然后把候选名单提交给委员会或小组讨论做出最终决定,最好不要轻易签订协议。

Field Visit 实地考察

在最终确定地点之前,实地考察非常重要。与会者可通过邮件、网络、旅游管理部门或其他途径获得各种场地信息,在此基础上再进行实地考察。

The Final Selection 最终选择

确定最终选择的场地。在选择中有需要注意的方面,当与会者完成实地考察后要尽快和各个考察地点取得联系。

1.3 The Content of Selecting the International Conference Center 国际会议会场选择的内容

When planners of international meetings are choosing a country to be the host country of the meeting, the organizers often face the following problems:

Is there a country willing to host the meeting? Not all countries have the

国际会议会场保障 | The Venue Selection of International Conference

same interests in all issues. The Nordic countries are interested in environmental issues. Japan is keen on human resources development. Developing countries are more concerned with bolstering their economies. Therefore, finding a number of states that are interested in the theme of the conference is, not always easy.

Some countries are often willing to host international conferences in order to improve their images, but some may have controversial domestic and foreign policies, some may have a negative image projected on to them by the outside world, some suffer slander from rival countries. Many delegates affected by public opinion at home and abroad would have reservations about, or opposition to, hosting an international conference.

Are countries prepared to host an international conference? Some countries are willing to host an international conference because it gives a positive image to the country, but due to the economic issues, poor infrastructure and even social unrest, they cannot guarantee the safety of the conference participants. Such countries are often excluded from consideration. Inability to raise sufficient funds can also make some countries abandon their plans to host an international conference.

Is there too much competition inside or outside the country? Even having the above three conditions, the international meeting planners sometimes also face a difficult competitive relationships between players. Different interest groups, geographical regions, and countries often fight over an important international conference and the competition is often harsh.

From the above four points of view, international meeting organizers have a limited number of available options when determining which country will host the meeting.

If the choice of a country is more concerned with political factors, when the organizers choose a city, they pay more attention to the natural environment, urban material conditions, and cultural conditions. This is to ensure that the meeting can be held in a beautiful, comfortable and convenient environment. The planners focus is on the following:

Access to the outside world, such as whether there are many flights. Because most of the participants abroad are flying in from inside and outside the border the number of routes and flights available to passengers is important. Planners should also concern themselves with telephone and fax reception.

The soundness of the city's infrastructure refers to whether there is sufficient water and power, the city traffic is convenient, etc. Without these basic guarantees, the events of the conference are bound to be affected.

The health and safety conditions of the city must be considered in order to protect the health and safety of the participants. A city that has serious pollution, epidemic diseases, violence, or conflicts should not be selected.

These conditions are generally guaranteed in the modern metropolises, they are more difficult to determine in small and medium-sized cities. Developing countries must make great efforts to create favorable conditions to attract international conferences to their countries. The more advanced developing countries have a particular interest in hosting international conferences on high value-added industries, so as to boost their own economic prosperity.

International conferences have a tendency to consistently return to certain cities.

Planners need to consider whether the hotel's location is conveniently located, service quality is good, conference facilities are good, and whether the venue has past experiences of an international conference.

When it comes to quality of service, people often think of the quality of catering. This is important, but one also cannot ignore service standardization and foreign language training. Service standardizations must conform to certain rules.

Conference facilities must be of great importance to the meeting planners when consider using the hotel to host a meeting. The hotel must be equipped to satisfy the needs of an international conference. Therefore, the organizers must identify that the hotel can satisfy the requirements of the conference facilities

The Choice of the Country 国家的选择

国际会议的策划者在选择某个国家作为会议东道国时往往面临以下问题：

（1）是否所有与会者对所有的问题都同样感兴趣？不同的国家有不同的侧重。北欧国家对环境问题兴趣更浓，日本热衷于人力资源开发，而发展

国际会议会场保障 | The Venue Selection of International Conference

中国家更关心改变经济落后。因此,要找到若干个对某一主题都感兴趣的国家并从中选择,实非易事。

(2) 是否所有国家的与会者都愿前去?有些国家为打开关系、树立形象,往往愿意承办国际会议,但有的可能因内外政策而声名狼藉,有的因外界刻意渲染而形象欠佳,有的则因敌手的造谣中伤而蒙受污损。许多代表,慑于国内外舆论,对在此类国家举行国际会议都会有保留意见或持反对立场。

(3) 是否具备承办国际会议的条件?有些国家有意承办国际会议,对外形象也较好,但经济落后,基础设施陈旧,甚至可能社会动荡,安全难有保证。这样的国家往往也被排除在考虑之外。有些国家筹措不到充分经费也会使其知难而退。

(4) 选择时关系能否能够处理得当?即使以上三个条件都具备,国际会议的策划者有时也面临难以处理的竞争关系。不同的利益集团、地理区域和国家常常为争夺一个重要的国际会议而打破了头。如果与会者把承办权交给了发达国家,发展中国家可能不悦;交给了拉美国家,亚洲国家可能皱眉。

从以上四点看来,国际会议的策划者在确定在哪个国家开会时,选择余地是较小的。

The Choice of the City 城市的选择

如果说国家的选择更多地考虑了政治因素,那么国际会议的策划者在选择城市时,更多地注重城市的自然环境、物质条件及人文状况,这是为了保证会议能在尽可能优美、宽松、便利的环境中举行。策划者关心的有:

(1) 拟议中的城市同外界的交通通信条件,譬如是否有较多的航线和航班。因为国外的与会者绝大多数是乘坐飞机参会。如航线多、航班密,旅客的选择余地就大,受滞阻的风险就小。同国外的电话、传真联系是否畅通,在会议期间与派出国能否保持正常联系,也是策划者应该考虑的内容。

(2) 该城市基础设施的健全程度。这是指水、电供应是否充足,市内交通是否方便等。没有这些基本保证,工作和生活都必然要受影响。

(3) 该城市的安全、卫生状况。考虑这些问题是为了保障与会者的人身安全和身体健康。一个暴力充斥、冲突迭起、污染严重、疫病流行的城市难以入选。

这些条件在现代化大都市一般都有保证,中小城市则难以保证。对发展中国家来说,它们尤需做出更大的努力,为吸引国际会议在本国举行创造条件。较为先进的发展中国家也把国际会议看作有高附加值的产业,借以推动本国经济发展。

The Choice of Hotel 酒店的选择

酒店所在的地段是否适中,服务质量是否高,会议设施是否齐全,有无举办国际会议经验,都是策划者所要考虑的。

酒店服务质量,包括服务人员的待客态度和勤快程度,以及工作的规范化和外语训练问题都是需要考量的方面。

会议设施也是会议策划者所看重的。借用酒店开会就要看酒店能否满足会议举办的设施要求。

2. Case Study
案例分析

2.1 Case Summary 案例概述

本章选择中外两个案例来阐述国际会议会场保障相关问题。第一则英文案例奥斯卡颁奖典礼上的会场服务。第二则中文案例反映的是在中国举办的国际会议的会场服务问题。通过这两则案例,读者可以明确国内外在举办国际会议时的通则和差异之处。

2.2 2015 Tokyo International Anime Fair

Case Guide-Reading 案例导读

This case is based on the venue arrangement of Academy Awards Ceremony. With the elements of the numerous procedures of this event, it examines the amount of work about the ceremony preparation for the reader.

The 87th Academy Awards ceremony, presented by the Academy of Motion Picture Arts and Sciences (AMPAS), will honor the best films of 2014 and will take place February 22, 2015, at the Dolby Theatre in Hollywood, Los Angeles beginning at 5:30 p.m. PST (8:30 p.m. EST/01:30 UTC)...

国际会议会场保障 | The Venue Selection of International Conference

Schedule

Date	Event
Saturday, November 8, 2014	The Governors Awards
Wednesday, December 3, 2014	Screen credits and music submissions due
Monday, December 29, 2014	Nominations voting begins 8:00 a.m. PST (11:00 a.m. EST)
Thursday, January 8, 2015	Nominations voting ends 5:00 p.m. PST (8:00 p.m. EST)
Thursday, January 15, 2015	Nominations announced 5:30 a.m. PST (8:30 a.m. EST)
Monday, February 2, 2015	Nominees luncheon
Friday, February 6, 2015	Final voting begins 8:00 a.m. PST (11:00 a.m. EST)
Saturday, February 7, 2015	Scientific and Technical Awards
Tuesday, February 17, 2015	Final voting ends 5:00 p.m. PST (8:00 p.m. EST)
Sunday, February 22, 2015	Ceremony begins 4:00 p.m. PST (7:00 p.m. EST)

...

PARKING

　　Entrances on Highland Avenue and Orange Drive. Effective January 1, 2015, parking rates are as follows: $2.00 for up to 2 hours with validation from participating retailers and restaurants $2.00 for up to 4 hours with validation from participating cinemas. $1.00 for every 15 minutes thereafter. Daily maximum is $15.00. Flat $15.00 rate after 10pm on Thursday, Friday and Saturday...

BOX OFFICE INFORMATION

　　...

EQUAL ACCESS INFORMATION

...

ANIMALS

Service animals are permitted at Dolby Theatre. The ADA defines a service animal as any guide dog, signal dog, or other animal individually trained to provide assistance to an individual with a disability...

If you have any questions about service animals or any other type of assistance animals, you may contact Dolby Theatre's event services department at 323-308-6375.

Please alert the theatre of any special needs at the time of your ticket purchase.

ARRIVAL

Dolby Theatre typically opens to the public one hour prior to the performance. Plan on arriving at least 30 minutes prior to the performance. Traffic in and around Hollywood can be congested at times, so you'll want to allow yourself plenty of time to get here, find parking, use the restroom and purchase concessions before the event begins. Ushers will direct you to your seat and are happy to answer any questions you may have about the theatre's amenities.

CELL PHONE & CAMERA USAGE

Dolby Theatre asks that you turn off or silence all noise-making electronics, text-messaging devices and cell phones during the performance. Taking pictures and video recording is prohibited inside the theatre.

CHILDREN

All persons entering the theatre, including babes in arms, must have a ticket. Please carefully consider whether a performance is appropriate for your child before planning to attend. Also, please be aware that disruptive patrons, including children, will not be allowed to remain in the theatre. Be considerate of others in the audience and of your child's comfort.

国际会议会场保障 | The Venue Selection of International Conference

COAT CHECK

A complimentary coat check is available on Lobby 2 of the theatre. Please note that backpacks and other, large bags are not permitted into the theatre.

DRESS CODE

Dolby Theatre had no formal dress code, and we encourage you to wear whatever makes you feel comfortable... However, please note that chains and spiked jewelry are not permitted inside the theatre. When in doubt, business casual is always appropriate. In addition, please consider the effects of strong perfumes and colognes on those seated around you.

EMERGENCY CONTACT

It is suggested patrons leave seat locations with baby sitters, answering services or other individuals who may need to contact them in the event of an emergency.

Administration (Mon—Fri, 8 AM—5 PM): 323-308-6300

Security (during most events): 323-308-6344

Box Office (during most public, ticketed events): 323-308-6369

FOOD & BEVERAGE

There are bars located in each lobby of Dolby Theatre where various soft drinks, mixed drinks, wine and beer may be purchased ...Dolby Theatre is proud to partner with Wolfgang Puck Catering as its exclusive food & beverage provider. Outside food & beverage, including water, is not permitted.

...

LOST & FOUND

Dolby Theatre's event services department oversees and manages any items left behind. Items considered "lost & found" will be kept secured in our security office for up to 30 days. If you have lost an item at Dolby Theatre, please call 323-308-6300.

> **LOUD TALKING & DISRUPTIONS DURING PERFORMANCES**
>
> Disruptions are not tolerated. If anyone disturbs the audience or interferes with the performance, the patron will be required to leave with no refund forthcoming.
>
> **RESTROOMS**
>
> Men's & women's restrooms are available on every lobby level of the theatre.
>
> **SECURITY**
>
> The following items are not permitted in Dolby Theatre. Bag checks are regularly conducted, and any guest attempting to enter the facility with such items will be asked to return that item to their vehicle.
>
> - Outside food & beverage.
>
> - Any type of weapon or item that can be used as a weapon (including pocket knives, chains and spiked jewelry.)
>
> - Laser pointers or any other item that may be considered disruptive to the performers or other audience members.
>
> **SMOKING**
>
> Smoking is strictly prohibited anywhere inside Dolby Theatre.

Analysis and Summary 分析概要

This case is selected from the venue arrangement of 87th Academy Awards Ceremony which indicates the outline of on-site service for this event. In this case, the information on schedule, emergency as well as lost & found and the relevant requirement for the audience are concerned by the planner. This case can be recognized as the model of the venue arrangement.

Questions 思考题

1. What is the composition for venue arrangement in this conference?
2. Compared with conferences at home, what are the differences in the venue arrangement for this conference?

2.3 重塑蓝天：空气质量管理国际研讨会

Case Guide-Reading 案例导读

本文属于一则有关国际会议会场保障的中文案例。在该案例中较为详细地阐述了国际会议会场布置、危机管控、设备、实务和票务等诸多方面的信息。通过对本案例的学习，读者可以较为全面地掌握国内举办国际会议时会场保障的基本内容。

> 2013年11月16日，能源基金会主办的"重塑蓝天：空气质量管理国际研讨会"在北京举行。200多位业界领导、专家、学者和媒体参与会议，针对中国当前所面临的空气质量问题，从宏观战略、区域防治和行业政策等方面展开深入讨论，提出应对方案。
>
> 该会议的会场保障工作由某公司担任，该公司提供了如下方案。
>
> **会议规划**
>
> 1. 场地规划
>
> ……
>
> 2. 基调处理
>
> 总体设计的基调包括造型基调、色彩基调、文风基调和动势基调。
>
> 3. 进度安排
>
> ……
>
> 4. 材料计划
>
> ……
>
> 5. 经费概算
>
> 包括劳务制作、场地租金、展具制作租赁、动力计费、安全防范、宣传广告以及交通食宿、新闻发布、工作人员的其他费用等。它是根据会议规模、设计档次、施工条件、管理能力以及外部环境而分别列出概算。
>
> **会议用车**
>
> ……

会场布置

　　1. 眉毛形式样

　　这种布置将两排椅子按月牙形相对而设,每排各放置5把。……值得注意的是,这种布置给那些穿短裙或裙子的女性一种容易走光的隐忧。

　　2. 多轮实惠的鸡尾酒

　　咖啡馆式的布置配上几轮小型的鸡尾酒,每轮都在主讲人和大屏周围摆放三个座位。这种形式适合各种类型的培训和思考讨论活动。……

　　3. 休息厅式样

　　虽然这种布置不利用发挥集体讨论,但有利于舒缓情绪、较随意的反映演讲人所说的话,或者一般性讨论活动。这种安排非常适合以专家为中心的单向演讲方式。

　　4. 播客式座位安排

　　这种布置有两张6尺长、类似课桌的桌子相对而设,在每张桌子一边摆放三张座位并在每排尾端都各摆放一张。……

　　5. 教室型

　　也就是戏院式或课桌式,是采用得最多的一种形式,它适用于以传达情况、指示为目的的会议,这时与会者人数比较多、而且与会者之间不需要讨论、交流意见。……

　　6. 圆桌或椭圆形桌子

　　……

　　7. 长形方桌

　　……

摄像问题

　　1. 机器通电无动作、无图像
　　2. 旋转时摄像机图像丢失
　　3. 摄像机不受遥控器控制
　　4. 摄像机在使用中自检无法进行或是伴有噪声

设备保障

　　我们为您提供专业的设施设备,电脑、投影仪及屏幕、复印机、打印

国际会议会场保障 | The Venue Selection of International Conference

> 机、传真机、音视频会议系统、同声传译系统、会场速记设备、电视机、舞台设计搭建、音响设备、各种灯具等,我们的设备均为世界一流品牌,并且定期更新,以保持最佳效果。
>
> **事务保障**
>   我们为客户提供专业秘书服务人员、翻译、勤杂、临时采购、临时司乘、向导等服务,用我们细心专业的服务为客户排除后顾之忧,为客户会议顺利进行锦上添花。
>
> **票务保障**
>   我公司为客户提供票务代理服务,为您的行程安排提供多个方案以供您选择,只要您有需要,我们当第一时间为您提供票务服务和咨询服务,为您出行提供便捷。

Analysis and Summary 分析概要

　　该案例选取一个中文国际会议作为样本,较为全面地展现了国内举办国际会议的会场保障工作。由该案例可以看出,国内有关单位进行国际会议会场服务时,较为重视会议规划、会议布置、危机管控等内容。该案例是国内有关单位举办国际会议时会场服务的基本内容,具有一定的代表性。

Questions 思考题

1. 在该案例中,会场服务由哪几个方面组成?呈现何种特色?

2. 在该案例中,国际会议会场保障与一般国外举办的国际会议的会场保障有何差异?

2.4 Case Comparison 案例对比

会议名称	重塑蓝天：空气质量管理国际研讨会	87th Academy Awards Ceremony
会场布置		
危机管控	1. 火灾 2. 恐怖袭击 3. 自然灾害 4. 医疗突发事件	It is suggested patrons leave seat locations with baby sitters, answering services or other individuals who may need to contact them in the event of an emergency. Administration (Mon-Fri, 8 AM — 5 PM): 323-308-6300 Security (during most events): 323-308-6344 Box Office (during most public, ticketed events): 323-308-6369 Patrons cannot be paged during a performance, but the House Manager will personally contact a seated patron in the event of an emergency when a seat location is provided.
会议设备	我们为您提供世界一流品牌，并且定期更新，以保持最佳效果的设备	Dolby Theater has a magnificently-designed interior, with a five-level theatre lobby. The main stage area of Dolby Theater is one of the largest in the US, measuring 120 feet wide and 75 feet deep.

国际会议会场保障 | The Venue Selection of International Conference

上述图片来自两个活动的主页

Analysis and Summary 分析概要

根据国际会议会场保障的基本内容，案例对比将所选择的中文和英文案例分块进行比较，以突显中外进行国际会议会场保障各项工作中的异同。

Questions 思考题

1. 通过上述两个案例的学习，可否明确国际会议会场保障的主要工作？
2. 上述两份国际会议会场保障在主要内容上有何异同？
3. 上述两份国际会议会场保障的主要内容有何内在联系？

3. Supplementary Reading
拓展阅读

3.1 2010 South Africa FIFA World Cup

The 2010 FIFA World Cup was the 19th FIFA World Cup, the world championship for men's national association football teams. It took place in South Africa from 11 June to 11 July 2010. The bidding process for hosting the tournament finals was open only to African nations; in 2004, the international football federation, FIFA, selected South Africa over Egypt and Morocco to become the first African nation to host the finals.

The matches were played in 10 stadiums in nine host cities around the country, with the final played at the Soccer City stadium in South Africa's largest city, Johannesburg. Thirty-two teams were selected for participation via a worldwide qualification tournament that began in August 2007. In the first round of the tournament finals, the teams competed in round-robin groups of four teams for points, with the top two teams in each group proceeding. These 16 teams advanced to the knockout stage, where three rounds of play decided which teams would participate in the final.

In the final, Spain, the European champions, defeated third-time finalists the Netherlands 1—0 after extra time, with Andrés Iniesta's goal in the 116th minute giving Spain their first world title, becoming the eighth nation to win the tournament, and the first European nation to win the tournament outside its home continent. As a result of their win, Spain represented the World in the 2013 FIFA Confederations Cup. Host nation South Africa, 2006 champions Italy and 2006 runners-up France were all eliminated in the first round of the tournament. It was the first time that the hosts were eliminated in the first round. New Zealand with their three draws were the only undefeated team in the tournament, but were also eliminated in the first round.

Host Selection

Africa was chosen as the host for the 2010 World Cup as part of a short-lived policy, abandoned in 2007, to rotate the event among football confederations. Five African nations placed bids to host the 2010 World Cup: Egypt, Morocco, South Africa and a joint bid from Libya and Tunisia.

Following the decision of the FIFA Executive Committee not to allow co-hosted tournaments, Tunisia withdrew from the bidding process. The committee also decided not to consider Libya's solo bid as it no longer met all the stipulations laid down in the official List of Requirements.

The winning bid was announced by FIFA president SeppBlatter at a media conference on 15 May 2004 in Zürich; in the first round of voting South Africa received 14 votes, Morocco received 10 votes and Egypt no votes. South Africa, which had narrowly failed to win the right to host the 2006 event, was thus awarded the right to host the tournament. Having successfully campaigned for South Africa to be granted host status, an emotional Nelson Mandela raised the FIFA World Cup Trophy.

During 2006 and 2007, rumours circulated in various news sources that the 2010 World Cup could be moved to another country. Franz Beckenbauer, Horst R. Schmidt and, reportedly, some FIFA executives, expressed concern over the planning, organization, and pace of South

国际会议会场保障 | The Venue Selection of International Conference

Africa's preparations. FIFA officials repeatedly expressed their confidence in South Africa as host, stating that a contingency plan existed only to cover natural catastrophes, as had been in place at previous FIFA World Cups.

According to the news, Johannesburg was criticized for local power cuts during the World Cup. About 90,000 new tickets have been put on the market, including seats at the previously sold-out final and semi-finals, causing a new rush by South Africans. Some people had been queuing for more than 24 hours to get tickets but when the system opened it immediately collapsed, as it did last month when over-the-counter sales first began in South Africa.

Blank-Filling

Directions: Complete each brackets with appropriate words or phrases from the passage.

The 2010 South Africa FIFA World Cup was played in 10 (   ) in nine host cities. Thirty-two teams were selected for (   ) through a worldwide qualification tournament. In the first round of the tournament finals, the teams competed in four teams for points, with the two teams in each group proceeding. These 16 teams advanced to the knockout stage, where three rounds of play (   ) which teams would participate in the final.

Questions and Answers

Directions: In this part there is one question. You need to answer the question based on the words or phrases from the passage.

According to this article, what are the problems in 2010 South Africa FIFA World Cup?

3.2 巴西世界杯

巴西圣保罗作为2014世界杯开幕式举办地的圣保罗竞技场依然没有完工，此时距离世界杯开幕仅剩下两个月不到的时间。圣保罗竞技场世界杯期间将举办包括揭幕战巴西VS克罗地亚在内的6场比赛，能容纳70000名观众。世界杯结束后球场规模将缩小至45000个

191

席位。

　　据悉，在圣保罗举行的巴西世界杯开幕式已进入倒计时阶段，距离开幕仅剩28天。

　　据报道，此次世界杯将在巴西的12个城市进行。但因事故造成足球赛场工程大幅延期的情况相继发生。截至15日，圣保罗市、有日本队比赛的库亚巴市、库里奇巴市，这3座城市的体育场均未完成建设，发展为史无前例的事态。

　　期间，此次世界杯的揭幕球场圣保罗体育场内，从早上开始就有大型卡车频繁出入，设立球场看台及安装看台座椅的工作还在持续。

　　球场的建设已临近国际足联的交付期限，但尾声工作仍在紧锣密鼓地进行。另一方面，巴西迎接来自世界各国球迷的准备工作也在顺利进行中。

　　距离巴西世界杯开幕还有11天，然而巴西世界杯开幕式的主球场仍未完工，巴西国内的抗议声也是不断。

阅读上述三则新闻报道，回答问题

1. 场馆建设作为申办世界杯时的重大承诺，项目延期对于本次世界杯比赛有何影响？

2. 国际会议是东道主展现本国风采的绝佳时机，场馆建设延期对于巴西的国际声誉有何影响？

国际会议会场保障 | The Venue Selection of International Conference

Exercises
课后练习

1. 阅读材料,回答问题。

> 2014年巴西举办金砖国家学术论坛时,当地政府高度重视,特地临时开辟市政厅用于相关学术活动。因为会场为临时改建而来,在会议进行时,巴西、俄罗斯、南非、印度和中国学者在用幻灯片进行学术研讨时,多次发生激光翻页器失灵的情况。
>
>
>
> 因为此次学术会议工作语言为英语,而会场工作人员母语并非英语,对于会场发生的紧急情况多有处理不及时,影响了正常的会议进程。

(1)根据所提供的材料,分析此次会场选择的问题何在。

(2)根据所学知识,在进行国际会议选址时,如何规避案例中出现的问题?

2. 阅读材料,回答问题。

> Conference Selection Ltd. is an internationally renowned Meeting and Conference venue finding Agency. From our inception in 1989, we rapidly became a major force within the venue finding industry and now handle in excess of 250 groups each year.
>
> During this period we have built a strong reputation for integrity and professionalism with both our clients and venues in the UK and Internationally. We take great pride in having built close working relationships with clients who have used our services for many years. We feel this has been due to our ability to offer a personal and expert approach to our client's needs.
>
> The Company is now able to offer a complete finding service to clients in both the UK and overseas, from recommending and locating suitable conference venues for meetings, conferences and seminars, to devising and operating Group Travel programmes for groups of 10 to 2000 world-wide.
>
> The services offered by Conference Selection cover two specific areas of our industry; International venue finding and Overseas Group Travel.

Questions and Answers

Directions: In this part there is one question. You need to answer the question based on the words or phrases from the passage.

What is the positive influence of the professional conference selection company for the international venue arrangement?

The Security of International Conference
国际会议安保

Overview
内容概览

Security issues cannot be ignored for public event. For international conference, the planner must firstly determine whether there is a need to carry out security plan and have security personnel on site. This should be determined according to the nature, size, content of the meeting, and level of participants. Once the organizer determines that there is a need for security, A well-developed security program should put into place.

国际会议的安保问题不容忽视。对于国际会议组织者而言,首先要根据会议的性质、规模、内容、参会人员的级别来确定会议是否需要开展安保工作。一旦确定需要安保工作,应及时制订周密的安保方案。

1. Basic Knowledge
基础知识

1.1 The Introduction of Security 安保基础

Security originally refers to the safety and peace, which regards acts such as guarding key political figures or defending of key activities as security. Security is now ubiquitous in every place so as to strengthen crime prevention efforts.

International conference security is put into place in order to ensure the smooth convening of an international conference, the development of a corresponding security program, and the process of implementing that program.

Security 安保

安保,原指安全、平安,使平安无事。现在各国警察把保卫保护重点人物或保卫重点活动等行为称为安保。现在安保工作已经深入各种大型活动,通过安保工作,预防犯罪,保障安全。

The Security of International Conference 国际会议安保

国际会议安保是指为了保证国际会议的顺利召开而制定相应的安全保障方案并加以执行的过程。

1.2 The Measures of Security Plan 制订安保计划的步骤

The sizes and levels of security solutions should be based on the importance of the meeting's attendees.

In developing a security plan, the special nature of this international conference should be taken into account. An appropriate security program in accordance with the special nature of the meeting can be developed.

Conference Location 会议定位

对国际会议有一个准确的定位,明确此次国际会议属于政治性会议、经济性会议还是文化性会议。

Determine the Size 确定规模

根据参加会议人员的重要性制定不同规模和级别的安保方案。

Particularity 特殊性

在制定安保方案时,还要考虑到此次国际会议的特殊性。特殊性主要与此次会议的时间、地点、和所采取的方法有所关联。由会议的特殊性制定相应的安保方案。

1.3 Security Program 安全保障方案

Security programs generally have two options: one is a permanent security strategy; the second is an emergency security plan.

Security working programs mainly involve the following arrangements: conference venue security work, security area, security personnel, and security forces.

In order to properly protect the convening of the meeting and to prevent

国际会议安保 | The Security of International Conference

intentional or deliberate acts of sabotage of the conference activities set up a buffer along the periphery of the meeting venue. Surrounding road traffic control should be arranged by police; it is necessary to set security buffers, which prevent malicious unrelated persons to from entering, avoid conflicts, reduce the risk of the occurrence of security incidents as well. In addition to security staffs and other staffs, unrelated persons are prohibited from entering the buffer zone, and the audience should line up single-file to go through security checkpoints.

According to the size of the meeting and the nature of participants, it is import to take appropriate security measures. To ensure the safety of the meeting, all non-staff at the work site must undergo security checks. Those who do not cooperate should be reported to the head of security; the ones who break in should be to taken away from the scene by security personnel, and dealt with by the police.

It is common to equip each site with emergent personnel plans, emergency exits, fire extinguishers, and a location map.

Emergency rescue plans are plans put in place after an explosion, fire, power failure, or conflict.

安全保障方案一般有两种，一是常设性安保方案，二是紧急安保方案。

Security Working Program 安全工作方案

安全工作方案主要涉及以下几个方面的安排。

Venue Security Work 会场内工作安保

第一，会议场地安保工作，设定安保工作领导小组，领导小组具体到个人。第二，对安保区域进行划分。第三，设定安保人员及标志。第四，安保力量部署。

Buffer Security 治安缓冲区安保

为了保障会议的正常召开，防止蓄意破坏会议活动的行为，在会议场地外围设置缓冲区。周边道路交通管制，由公安机关处置；设置治安缓冲区，防止无关人员的恶意进入，避免发生冲突，降低发生治安事件的概率，除安保和工作人员外，严禁无关人员进入缓冲区，观众通过隔离依次排队安检。

Admission Ticket Checking and Security Screening Measures 入场人员票证检查及安全检查措施

根据会议规模、参会人群性质,采取相应的安检标准。禁止参会人员带入违禁品,并实施不低于50%的开包检查。为保证会议的安全,所有进入场地的非工作人员必须接受安全工作检查,对不配合者,上报领导小组,对强硬闯入的,请求现场保安人员予以支援,带离现场,并交由现场公安机关处理。

Meeting Fire Safety Measures 会议消防安全措施

向现场每位安保人员发放突发事件应急预案、安全出口、灭火器位置图。

Public Order Maintenance and Personnel Counseling 现场秩序维护及人员疏导

维护现场秩序,疏导各参会人员的活动范围与区域。

Emergency Rescue Plan 突发事件应急救援方案

对于突发事件应急救援方案,一定要先制定总负责人和场地负责人。突发事件应急救援方案涉及爆炸事件发生后、发生火灾后、发生停电后、发生冲突后、场地人员超过核定容量等意外情况的方案。

1.4 Emergency Treatment in Meeting 会议中突发事件的处理

Hotels, convention centers and other agencies generally have their own emergency measures, but they are usually more willing to work with meeting planners and planning agencies to share emergency action plans.

Fire can break out rapidly and violently, and there is a need for proper fire safety equipment to control the situation. The hotel room is generally attached to a fire escape. It is very important for participants to understand the fire emergency action plan how to exit the building quickly and safely. . Include the fire emergency action plan in the program book or distribute to participants as additional materials.

After 2001, terrorism is no longer an isolated phenomenon. Many public agencies have developed appropriate strategies to deal with such events. These strategies are not intended for meetings in hotels or convention center, but these could also become targets of terrorist attacks. Since the situation is difficult to

国际会议安保 | The Security of International Conference

predict, the security and risk management requirements increase. It is best that organizers enact emergency action plans, and have targeted staff training, so that when an emergency occurs, they can work together with participants. Organizers can also have cooperation with hotel employees and law enforcement, and act in accordance with their instructions.

Another emergency beyond the organizer's control is natural disasters. Hurricanes, storms, earthquakes, and forest fires are all typical natural disasters. To prepare for natural disasters, the organizers must have a strategy and plant to evacuate attendee safely. They also must develop a recovery plan and consider how to compensate for the loss. Event organizers should not just focus on general commercial insurance; other types of insurance can also very useful.

There should also be a medical emergency action plan, as attendees may have no signals before a heart attack, some people suddenly have intense allergic reactions to food, and diabetics may fall into a coma. Meeting planners should take these circumstances into account and communicate with the hotel medical sector in advance; they should be familiar with nearby hospitals and medical institutions. In addition, the staff can be trained in artificial respiration or cardiopulmonary resuscitation rescue method. Many hotels and agencies require all personals, from general managers to the doormen, to take cardiopulmonary resuscitation and rescue resuscitation courses. The purpose of these courses is to make everyone understands that saving lives is the responsibility of every citizen.

酒店、会展中心等机构一般都有各自的应急措施，他们当然也更愿意与会议策划者和策划机构合作，共享措施，共担风险。

Fire 火灾

火灾来势迅速而且凶猛，需要有适当的灭火器械或相应的工具，才能控制住局面。酒店的客房内一般都贴有火灾逃离须知。虽然与会者曾经看过多次了，但作为大会的策划者和组织机构，仍然有必要让与会者了解。把这些注意事项打印在计划书中或作为附加材料发放到与会者手中，就会减少不少不必要的损失。

Terrorist Attacks 恐怖袭击

2001年后，人类对恐怖主义已经不再陌生。许多酒店和公共机构已经制定了相应的对策来处理此类事件。这些对策并非针对会议组织机构或举办会议的酒店或会展中心，而是因为它们有可能成为恐怖组织袭击的目标。由于情况难以预测，安全和风险管理的要求也随之提高。主办方最好制订一些应急行动计划，并对员工进行针对性的培训，以便当紧急情况发生时，他们可以和与会者共同应对。主办方还可以和酒店员工以及执法部门合作，按照他们的指令行事。

Natural Disasters 自然灾害

另一种在组织者控制能力之外的紧急事件就是自然灾害。飓风、暴风雨、地震、森林大火都是典型的自然灾害。面对自然灾害，组织者无计可施。唯一能做的就是制订出一个恢复计划以及考虑如何弥补损失。在这种情况下，保险就是救生员。不要只是关注一般的商业保险，其他种类的保险也是很有用处的。

Medical Accidents 医疗事件

一个人心脏病发作可能没有任何预兆。有些人吃了过敏的食物后，身上会突然出现皮疹并且呼吸道发生阻塞。糖尿病人有可能会陷入昏迷。这些医疗突发事件的时间、地点以及情形总是不可控制的。

会议策划者在策划会议时应该考虑到这些情形，可以和酒店医疗部门事先做好沟通，同时要熟悉会议场地附近医院及医疗机构的情况。另外，让工作人员学会人工呼吸或心肺救助复苏方法也是一个明智之举。许多酒店和机构要求从总经理到门童在内的所有人员都要上人工呼吸和心肺救助复苏方法课程。这些课程的目的是让所有人明白，挽救生命是每个公民的职责；且当医疗事件发生时，可迅速处置，减少损失。

2. Case Study 案例分析

2.1 Case Summary 案例概述

本章选取中外案例来阐述国际会议安保的相关问题。第一则英文案例在于说明G20会议时，澳大利亚政府的安保举措。第二则案例意在说明中国在举办上海亚信峰会时的安保举措。

国际会议安保 | The Security of International Conference

2.2 2014 G20 Brisbane Summit Safety and Security Act (extract)

Case Guide-Reading 案例导读

This case is based on the security procedure of G20 Brisbane Summit. With the outline of the numerous aspects of this event, it examines the amount of work about the safety arrangement for the reader.

> **Part 7 Offences**
>
> **63 Prohibited item offences**
>
> (1) A person must not, without lawful excuse, possess a prohibited item in a security area. Maximum penalty—50 penalty units.
>
> (2) A person must not, without lawful excuse, attempt to take a prohibited item into a security area. Maximum penalty—50 penalty units.
>
> (3) A person must not, without lawful excuse, use a prohibited item in a way that it, something contained in it or on it or something produced by it, may enter a security area. Maximum penalty—100 penalty units.
>
> ...
>
> (4) The onus of proving lawful excuse under subsection (1), (2) or (3) is on the person claiming the lawful excuse.
>
> **64 Climbing onto, under, over or around barrier, etc.**
>
> (1) This section applies to any of the following things placed for a G20 purpose (a placed thing) ...
>
> (2) A person must not do any of the following in relation to a placed thing—
>
> ...
>
> Maximum penalty—50 penalty units.
>
> **65 Application of s 64 limited**
>
> Section 64 does not apply to— ...
>
> **66 Entering or climbing building or structure in view of security area with intent to cause injury, etc.**
>
> A person must not enter or climb a building or structure in view of a

security area with intent to do any or all of the following— ...

67 Lighting a fire in a security area

A person must not light a fire in a security area without lawful excuse, the onus of proving which is on the person. Maximum penalty— 100 penalty units.

68 Failing to comply with requirement to disclose personal details

(1) A person who is required to disclose the person's personal details under section 37(1) (b) or (2) (b) or 38(1) must comply with the requirement. Maximum penalty—10 penalty units.

(2) However, a person does not commit an offence under subsection (1) merely because the person fails to produce identification if the person has a lawful excuse for the failure.

(3) In this section—identification means— ...

69 Failing to comply with direction

(1) A person must not, without lawful excuse, fail to comply with a direction given by a police officer under this Act. Maximum penalty—50 penalty units.

(2) In a proceeding for an offence against this section, a direction given to a person or a group of persons is taken to have been heard and understood by the person or group, unless the contrary is proved.

70 Unauthorised entry to restricted area

A person must not enter or attempt to enter or remain in a restricted area unless the person has special justification to do so. Maximum penalty—50 penalty units.

71 Unauthorised entry to motorcade area

A person must not enter or attempt to enter or remain in a motorcade area unless the person has special justification to do so. Maximum penalty—50 penalty units.

国际会议安保 | The Security of International Conference

72 Prohibited person not to enter security area

A prohibited person must not enter, or attempt to enter, a security area. Maximum penalty—100 penalty units.

73 Unauthorised entry to security area by excluded person

An excluded person must not enter, or attempt to enter, a security area or part of a security area from which the person is excluded under the exclusion notice given to the person. Maximum penalty—100 penalty units

74 Interfering with any part of the G20 meeting

At any site where any part of the G20 meeting is held or takes place, a person must not— ...

75 Assaulting or obstructing appointed person

(1) A person must not assault or obstruct an appointed person exercising a power or performing a function under this Act. Maximum penalty—40 penalty units.

(2) In this section—obstruct includes hinder, resist and attempt to obstruct.

Part 8 Exemptions from particular offence provisions

76 Application of Transport Operations (Road Use Management) Act 1995

(1) Provisions of the Transport Operations (Road Use Management) Act 1995 about offences, other than sections 79 and 80, do not apply to the driver of a vehicle that is part of a motorcade under escort by a police officer.

(2) In this section— motorcade includes a vehicle being driven by a police officer escorting the motorcade.

77 Power to give emergency direction to disobey traffic provision

(1) For a G20 purpose, a police officer may give a direction in an emergency to a relevant person to disobey a traffic provision.

...

Analysis and Summary 分析概要

This case is selected from the safety and security acts of G20 Brisbane Summit which indicates the sophisticated work for this event. In this case, the information on complicated security law making is concerned by the planner. Those vast tasks were totally under the track of the law. This case can be recognized as the representative of the security plan for international conference.

Questions 思考题

1. What/which is new of this conference's security measures?
2. Compared with conferences at home, what are the differences in those security measures for this conference?

2.3 2014 上海亚信峰会

Case Guide-Reading 案例导读

本文属于一则有关国际会议安保的中文案例。该案例较为详细地阐述了国际会议会场布置、危机管控、设备、实务和票务等诸多方面信息。通过对本案例的学习，读者可以较为全面地掌握国内举办国际会议时会场保障的基本内容。

> 亚洲相互协作与信任措施会议（简称"亚信"）第47届联合国大会上倡议成立，1993年3月起作为论坛开始活动。目前是亚洲规模最大的多边安全论坛。
>
> 中国是2014年至2016年的亚信主席国。今年的亚信峰会将于5月20日至21日在上海举行……
>
> 成员数目:24个(……)
>
> 观察员数目:13个(……)
>
> 组织机构:
>
> 主席国
>
> ……2014年，中国将首次正式接任2014年至2016年亚信主席国，这是中国首次担任亚信主席国。
>
> 召开频率:四年一次
>
> 宗旨:通过制定旨在增进亚洲和平、安全与稳定的多边信任措施

国际会议安保 | The Security of International Conference

来加强合作。

安保工作：

亚信峰会首次在中国举办，也是亚信成立以来，参与国最多、规模最大、规格最高的一次盛会。会议期间，上海全市社会治安平稳有序，未发生重特大刑事、治安案（事）件、火灾事故和长时间、大面积道路交通拥堵。

亚信峰会安全顺利：守住边、稳住面、保住点，圆满实现安保目标

中央高度重视亚信峰会安保工作。中共中央政治局委员、中央政法委书记孟建柱，国务委员、公安部部长郭声琨亲自作安保工作动员，并在上海坐镇指挥。公安部副部长黄明、刘彦平等领导具体部署、协调推动安保措施细化落实。

上海市委、市政府将峰会安保工作作为整个保障筹备工作的核心和关键来抓。中共中央政治局委员、上海市委书记韩正，市委副书记、市长杨雄要求举全市之力，万无一失地做好峰会安保工作。上海亚信峰会保障筹备工作协调小组组长、市委常委、常务副市长屠光绍，市委常委、市委政法委书记姜平等领导实地检查指导安保工作。

上海公安机关和全体民警，闻令而动，勇担重任，以饱满的精神状态、扎实的工作措施迎接挑战。上海市副市长、公安局局长白少康向全市公安民警发出号令："要以最高标准、最强措施、最严要求，推进落实各项安保工作，确保峰会安全顺利举行。"

……

水陆空立体化防控：大门查、空中巡、街巷守，密织峰会安保网络

为顺利完成亚信峰会安保任务，上海市公安局努力构建立体化、全方位的安保体系，守住进沪通道，保持良好的社会治安秩序和城市公共安全，做到了"守住边、稳住面、保住点"，确保了亚信峰会期间，上海社会整体秩序平安有序，各项峰会安保工作顺利推进。

……

突发情况快速出击处置：组建125支快反机动队，实施跨警种联勤、警力叠加，实现警务模式升级

……

205

> 黄浦分局共有15支特种机动队,而在全市范围内,这种特种机动队共有125支。每支机动队有5到10人,由治安、交管、刑侦等不同警种民警组成。遇有突发情况,这支队伍可以在短时间内抵达现场,形成优势警力,快速处置。
>
> 应急处突特种机动队是上海市公安局为应对亚信峰会安保任务推出的警务模式创新之一。除此之外,上海市公安局整体布局,打破界限,实现警种间联勤联动,必要时实行警力叠加,下活了全市警力调配"一盘棋",全面构建起升级版的现代警务模式。
>
> 上海还启动地方公安与铁路公安联合武装巡逻。联合武装巡逻打破管辖界限,叠加巡逻防控,同时也实现了地方公安和铁路公安之间的信息互通。在上海南站,地方公安与铁路公安实现了视频互通……
>
> 在更高层面上,上海市公安局成立综合情报实战研判平台,多警种合成办公,数据库信息随时调用,实现大数据整合、大平台应用、大格局发布,为快速研判分析警情提供便利。
>
> **高效高质警务实现少扰民:游园不停、婚礼照办,交通管制精确、礼炮鸣放告知**
>
> 5月21日11时,上海豫园区域游人如织,一如平日。豫园内园,与会政要夫人们正在参观游览。一墙之隔的外围旅游与商业区不受影响,秩序井然。
>
> ……

Analysis and Summary 分析概要

该案例选取一个中文国际会议作为样本,较为全面地展现了国内举办国际会议的安保工作。由该案例可以看出,国内有关单位进行国际会议安保时,较为重视安保领导工作和群防群控。该案例是国内有关单位举办国际会议时安保工作的基本内容和方式,具有一定的代表性。

Questions 思考题

1. 在该案例中,会场安保由哪几个方面组成?呈现何种特色?

国际会议安保 | The Security of International Conference

2. 在该案例中,国际会议安保与一般国外举办国际会议时的安保有何差异?

2.4 Case Comparison 案例对比

会议名称	2014上海亚信峰会	2014 G20 Brisbane Summit Safety and Security Act (extract)
安保范围	以上海为主	Mainly in Brisbane
安保对象	与会领导人及随行人员生命财产安全	Persons attending the Group of Twenty leaders' summit in Brisbane in 2014 and other related meetings and events in Queensland in 2014, to ensure the safety of members of the community and to protect property during the hosting of the summit and other related meetings
安保人员	警察、武警官兵、部队、国安及保镖等	Police officers, non-State police officers and appointed persons with special powers
安保内容	亚信峰会安全顺利:守住边、稳住面、保住点,圆满实现安保目标 水陆空立体化防控:大门查、空中巡、街巷守,密织峰会安保网络 突发情况快速出击处置:组建125支快反机动队,实施跨警种联勤、警力叠加,实现警务模式升级 高效高质警务实现少扰民:游园不停、婚礼照办、交通管制精确、礼炮鸣放告知	• to promote the safety and security of persons attending any part of the G20 meeting; • to ensure the safety of members of the public from acts of civil disobedience in relation to any part of the G20 meeting; • to protect property from damage from civil disobedience in relation to any part of the G20 meeting; • to prevent acts of terrorism directly or indirectly related to any part of the G20 meeting; • to regulate traffic and pedestrian movement to ensure the passage of motorcades related to any part of the G20 meeting is not impeded.

Analysis and Summary 分析概要

根据国际会议安保的基本内容,案例对比将所选择的中文和英文案例分块进行比较,以突显中外进行国际会议安保各项工作中的异同。

Questions 思考题

1. 通过上述两个案例的学习,可否明确国际会议安保的主要工作?
2. 上述两份国际会议安保在主要内容上有何异同?
3. 上述两份国际会议安保的主要内容有何内在联系?

3. Supplementary Reading
拓展阅读

3.1 1972 Munich Olympics

The 1972 Summer Olympics, officially known as the Games of the XX Olympiad, was an international multi-sport event held in Munich, West Germany, from August 26 to September 11, 1972. The sporting nature of the event was largely overshadowed by the Munich massacre in which eleven Israeli athletes and coaches and a West German police officer were killed. Five Black September terrorists died.

The 1972 Summer Olympics were the second Summer Olympics to be held in Germany, after the 1936 Games in Berlin, which had taken place under the Nazi regime. Mindful of the connection, the West German Government was eager to take the opportunity of the Munich Olympics to present a new, democratic and optimistic Germany to the world, as shown by the Games' official motto, "Die HeiterenSpiele," or "the Happy Games."[citation needed] The logo of the Games was a blue solar logo (the "Bright Sun") by OtlAicher, the designer and director of the visual conception commission. The Olympic mascot, the dachshund "Waldi," was the first officially named Olympic mascot. The Olympic Fanfare was composed by Herbert Rehbein, a companion of Bert Kaempfert.

The Olympic Park (Olympiapark) is based on Frei Otto's plans and after the Games became a Munich landmark. The competition sites,

国际会议安保 | The Security of International Conference

designed by architect GüntherBehnisch, included the Olympic swimming hall, the Olympics Hall (Olympiahalle, a multipurpose facility) and the Olympic Stadium (Olympiastadion), and an Olympic village very close to the park. The design of the stadium was considered revolutionary, with sweeping canopies of acrylic glass stabilized by metal ropes, used on such a large scale for the first time.

Because some athletes was drunk and they sometimes got over the fence, the security personeels gradually became unresponsible, which gave the terrorists chances to get into the Israeli athelets' rooms.

During the terrorist acts, the police didn't pay attention to the call from the Olympics Village. An hour later, the director of the police was waked up and then they started to rescue.

Blank-filling

Directions: Complete each brackets with appropriate words or phrases from the passage.

The 1972 Summer Olympics were the second Summer Olympics to be held in Germany, after the 1936 Games in Berlin, which (   ) under the Nazi regime. The West German Government was eager to (   ) of the Munich Olympics to present a new Germany to the world.

The (   ) of the Games was a blue solar logo (the "Bright Sun") by OtlAicher, the designer and director of the conception commission. The Olympic (   ), the dachshund "Waldi", was the first officially named Olympic mascot. The Olympic Fanfare was composed by Herbert Rehbein, a companion of Bert Kaempfert.

Questions and Answers

Directions: In this part there is one question. You need to answer the question based on the words or phrases from the passage.

According to this article, what are the security problems in 1972 Munich Olympics?

3.2 国际会议安保模式

> 随着全球化时代的步伐加快,国际会议呈现更高的频次。在东道国的多方协调好,国际会议的安保工作日益迈向机制化的轨道。已经形成如下几个相对固定的内容:
>
> 建立强有力的安全保卫机构。在国家或区域层面建立起安全保卫领导和协调机构,统揽安保全局工作。
>
> 储备充足的警力。国际会议安保一般需要调配军队、警察甚至安全部门的特殊力量来共同实施,需要在常规会场和街面防控的同时,做好关键部位的安保工作。
>
> 划分安全区域。有些重大国际会议所在城市或敏感区域会划定禁飞区或禁行区,并在不同的区域实施不同级别的安全保障措施,做好防控层级,将安保力量投放到适宜的位置。
>
> 实施反恐演练。随着国际恐怖主义活动进入活跃期,国际会议安保工作需要针对恐怖袭击进行专项预案和安排,做到未雨绸缪。
>
> 施行特别警卫措施。针对不同嘉宾的属性,实行差异化警卫服务,确保会议要员安全。

问答题

阅读上述材料,回答问题。
当前国际会议的安全保卫工作主要有哪些方面的内容?

实例

结合与会者所了解的情况,历史上曾经发生过哪些国际会议安保悲剧?这些悲剧对当下国际会议的安全保卫工作有何启示?

国际会议安保 | The Security of International Conference

Exercises
课后练习

1. 阅读材料,回答问题。

> 2014亚信峰会对安保的要求非常高。按照中央统一要求、公安部统一部署,上海公安系统等与长三角地区通力合作,全力以赴保障峰会。同时,安保工作也得到了上海市民的广泛支持,全社会共同构筑起亚信的安保体系。
>
> 上海成立了亚信峰会交通行业安保工作领导小组,设港口码头、内河水运、道路危险货物运输、道路客运、道路保障、轨道交通、市境道口等专项工作组,制定了安保专项管控方案。
>
> 在与峰会相关的重点区域,上海警方加强部署特警、武警,实施叠加巡逻、动态备勤。在一些重要景观场所可以见到驾驶摩托车的巡逻警队和佩枪巡警等。上海、江苏、浙江海警部队500余名官兵,也加入了亚信峰会海上安保阵容。
>
> 上海共启用亚信峰会定点医疗保障医院18家,组建了60个医疗小组,14个专科医疗小组,4支专家队伍和45组配备监护型急救车的急救小组等参与峰会医疗保障,提供24小时全天候服务。距离会场较近的上海东方医院、浦南医院等已进行了多次应急救援演练。
>
> 此次共有30万名平安志愿者在公共场所、主要景观、道路,提供各类公益服务,倡导"服务亚信、奉献亚信,我参与,我快乐"的理念。

(1) 根据材料,分析亚信峰会安保策略与传统的安全保障有何区别。

(2) 在全球恐怖主义活跃的背景下,本届亚信峰会安保对于大型国际会议有何启发?

2. 观看电影《慕尼黑》,分析主办方在运动员安保方面存在的漏洞。

3. G-7 Summit: Huge Security Operation Around Castle Elmau, Germany

> ELMAU, Germany — World leaders including President Barack Obama will be guarded by 17,000 police officers when they arrive high in the southern German Alps for two days of meetings at the G7 summit this weekend.
>
> Located at more than 3,000 feet above sea level, Castle Elmau has created special challenges for organizers of this year's global conference, which begins on Sunday.
>
> The luxury hotel is surrounded by lush green fields, dense forests and Alpine mountains and has only with only one paved road leading up to it.
>
> Major highways are shut down and temporary border posts have been set up on at least one mountain trail in Bavaria's largest ever police operation.

(1) According to the above materials, why did the security budget increase rapidly for the recent G7 summit?

(2) With the increasing of security personnel, what changes could happen to the security concepts?

Reference
参考文献

Barbara J. Streibel. (2007). *Plan and Conduct Effective Meetings*. McGraw-Hill.

Getz, D. (2005). *Event Management and Event Tourism* (2nd ed). Cognizant.

Judy Allen. (2009). *Event Planning*. Wiley.

Marty Brounstein. (2012). *Running a Great Meeting: In a Day For Dummies*. Wiley.

MTD Training. (2010). *Running Effective Meetings*. Ventus Publishing ApS.

Patrick Dunne. (2005). *Running Board Meetings*. London and Sterling. VA.

Robert Finch Miller. and Marilyn Pincus. (2004). *Running a Meeting That Works*. Barron's.

Tony Rogers. (2008). *Conferences and Conventions: A Global Industry* (2nd ed). Elsevier Ltd.

Patti J. Shock, John M. Stefanelli. (2001). *On-Premise Catering: Hotels, Convention & Conference Centers, and Clubs*. John Wiley & Sons, Inc.

戴光全著:《重大事件对城市发展及城市旅游的影响研究》,中国旅游出版社,2005。

哈佛商学院编,王春颖译:《会议管理》,商务印书馆,2009。

胡伟:《会议管理》,东北财经大学出版社,2009。

欧阳国忠:《活动策划实战全攻略》,清华大学出版社,2013。

腾宝红:《会务主管日常管理工作技能与范本》,人民邮电出版社,2008。

文春英、刘新鑫著:《国际会议策划与筹办》,中国传媒大学出版社,2012。

徐虹著:《饭店企业核心竞争力研究》,旅游教育出版社,2004。

袁学娅:《中外酒店管理比较:入世后我国酒店管理如何同国际接轨》,辽宁科技出版社,2002。

张晓娟:《会展概论》,东北财经大学出版社,2008。

中国就业培训技术指导中心编:《秘书国家职业资格培训课程三级秘书》,中央广播电视大学出版社,2006。
李树梅:"会议现场服务技巧",载《经济研究导刊》,2010(26):284—285。
潘金宽、马小英:会务工作四要诀,载《会议论坛》,2006(3):36—37。
武少源:"国际会议餐饮活动的策划与实施",载《中国会展》,2008(1):217—219。
张是美:"会议工作应注重的几个细节",载《秘书工作》,2010(9):28。
张涛:"做好大型会务工作之我见",载《秘书工作》,2010(9):26—27。

网址

http://www.embok.org/

http://epms.net/